ANSWERS
FROM WITHIN

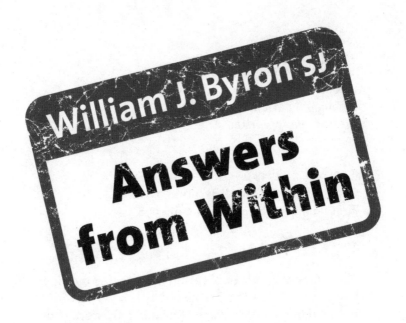

William J. Byron SJ

Answers from Within

**Spiritual Guidelines
for Managing
Setbacks in Work**

VERITAS

Published 2010 by
Veritas Publications
7–8 Lower Abbey Street
Dublin 1, Ireland
Email publications@veritas.ie
Website www.veritas.ie

ISBN 978 1 84730 215 1
Copyright © William J. Byron SJ, 2010
First Published by Macmillan in 1998

10 9 8 7 6 5 4 3 2 1

A catalogue record for this book is available from the British
Library.

Designed by Norma Prause-Brewer

Printed in the Republic of Ireland by ColourBooks Ltd, Dublin

Veritas books are printed on paper made from the wood pulp
of managed forests. For every tree felled, at least one tree is
planted, thereby renewing natural resources.

For Tom Donnelly, whose
personal and professional
integrity I admire; and to the
memory of Clif Brown,
whose life and death brought
Tom and me together in
faith and friendship

CONTENTS

Our very life depends on everything's
Recurring till we answer from within.
The thousandth time may prove the charm.

— Robert Frost, 'Snow'

INTRODUCTION

This is an abridged and revised version of a book that first appeared in 1998. It is written for men and women of faith, who may need a compass to keep themselves on track when things go wrong in the workplace. That seems to be happening more often now than when I first wrote, but then, as now, faith is the needle on the compass this book will recommend.

This is not a reference work meant to be consulted only when problems arise, as one might consult a computer user's manual. What is offered in these pages will work best if absorbed in quiet moments alone, at times when you can distance yourself from the inevitable stress, worry, and pressure that are part of every life and are certainly predictable parts of your own workplace life.

Franz Kafka once remarked that a book 'should serve as an ax for the frozen sea within us'. In your hands you are now holding an ax designed to cut into the sea of your soul, a literary ax meant to crack open the way for in-spiriting ideas that can be internalised and made a vital part of you. These ideas are principles of action, spiritual guidelines that will enable you to cope with setbacks in the workplace. These ideas will shape your answers from within, answers that only you can give to the questions that surround you.

Once internalised through prayer and reflection, these ideas can be carried with you everywhere you go. They are particularly potent allies in the workplace (and in the marketplace, where persons from one workplace interact with representatives of another).

These ideas can function as shields against stress, as signposts pointing towards spiritual solutions to personal on-the-job problems, and as reaffirmations of the relevance of religious faith to the working life. Once assimilated, these ideas become transformative and, thus transformed, you will become a person who encourages and empowers character-building virtuous actions in others.

CHANGES
There is a lot of talk these days about transforming the workplace, making it more humane and respectful of human dignity. That won't happen until individuals who go to work each day are themselves first transformed. That simple, undeniable fact points to the revolutionary potential of a spirituality suited to your workplace.

The change I have in mind has virtually nothing to do with organisational restructuring and just about everything to do with making a personal commitment to the search for purpose, both on and off the job.

HOW THIS BOOK IS STRUCTURED
This book is presented in three parts.

Part One offers an introduction to practical spirituality. This is background material, part of the equipment you need to deal with everyday problems. In Part One, you will find the basic material – the infrastructure, if you will – that supports all that will emerge by way of *Answers from Within*.

Part Two covers experiences that may best be classified as 'workplace wounds'. This part of the book deals with unpleasant realities where spirituality is not simply tested, but demonstrates its power to sustain believers who are willing to relate their faith commitments to their workplace responsibilities.

Part Three puts spiritual pillars, a supportive foundation, under the person whose faith perspective is wide enough to find God on the job. This section of the book opens the door of hope for those whose faith has stood the test of time.

PRACTICAL SPIRITUALITY

Workplace spirituality is the thread that runs through these pages. The focus is on practical spirituality, one grounded in a sense of vocation. You will know that you have found this type of spirituality when you have an awareness that you are 'called' to do what you do, Monday to Friday, nine to five (or later) – just as much as you are called to family responsibilities, and perhaps to membership in a faith community. Grasping a sense of 'being called' is not so difficult as you may at first suspect.

THE PAULINE CRITERIA

You will find outlined in the early part of this book the most important ideas supporting this type of spirituality. You will also find an explanation of how biblically-based virtues, which I call the Pauline Criteria, can function as spiritual guidelines. These nine virtues can serve as pillars of support when workplace stresses threaten to unbalance a life and derail a career. These virtues are:

¬ Love
¬ Joy
¬ Peace
¬ Patience
¬ Kindness
¬ Generosity
¬ Faithfulness
¬ Gentleness
¬ Self-control

These may not strike you at the moment as the stuff of a strategic plan for getting ahead in the world of work. But keep on reading!

AFFECTS

David E. Morrison, MD, founder of Morrison Associates, a business consulting firm in the USA, is a psychiatrist who works with organisational leaders and managers on issues related to workplace stress. He introduced me to the insights of the late Silvan S. Tompkins, whose writings on 'affects' influence the approach Dr Morrison takes to emotional issues that can enhance or impede effective work.

Following Tompkins (author of *Affect, Imagery, Consciousness*, Springer, 1962), Morrison identifies nine affects, or basic emotional responses, that will be elaborated upon later in this book. Only two of these affects are positive. One of those, 'Enjoyment-Joy', defines a culture that Morrison sees as both supportive of the nine virtues just listed and necessary for a healthy workplace.

The early portion of the book you are now holding also deals with the 'human predicament', an expression that suggests a troubling tension between matter and spirit, joy and sorrow, success and failure, a tension that will be felt in every human life. All too often, it appears, human beings spend the first half of their lives warming up and the second half wearing out. Just when it all appears to be coming together, there are indications that things are beginning to come apart. That's our predicament: our human condition. We never seem to be able to get life to the perfect point, and to keep it 'just right'.

DAY BY DAY

This book also encourages you to come to terms with the relevance of religious faith to normal, everyday working life. It highlights the relationship between the Sunday-centred preoccupations of believers and their Monday to Friday occupations. When faith-based spirituality becomes congregational, when individual faith is nourished by word and sacrament in community – exactly what happens in Sunday religious assemblies – something surfaces that can be carried over into Monday for the enrichment of life in the workplace.

The search for that 'something' leads towards a spirituality that is supportive of busy men and women who want to find a way for their commitments to God and work to become mutually reinforcing.

A SPECIFIC FAITH PERSPECTIVE

I take a Christian faith perspective in these pages and, from that perspective, I invite the reader to carry some of the 'boundary' questions of life into that zone of reflection where good Christians, who will inevitably experience some bad things in the workplace and elsewhere, have to search for meaning.

My personal faith commitment is Roman Catholic and my spirituality has been shaped by my six decades of life as a Jesuit. That background will be evident to you as this book unfolds – as will, I hope, my respect for other faith traditions.

Prayer is an integral part of my own spiritual life, and of this book as well. Ongoing conversation with God, or just listening to God, is essential to a well-grounded spiritual life. I hope you'll pause from time to time as you move through this book for that kind of conversation, that kind of listening.

How do I know what you might want to say to God? I don't. How do I know if you even wish to pause for prayer as you are moving through these pages? I don't. I just hope you will.

APPLICATIONS

An important part of my purpose in writing this book is to help you apply spirituality to the realities of workplace life, especially those realities best described by the 'Bard of Avon' centuries ago as the 'slings and arrows of outrageous fortune'. This book will offer you short, to-the-point discussion of familiar workplace wounds – those often unintended, sometimes deliberate, blows that can strike at any time. Nursing your wounds is not the way to maintain balance and move forward. Drawing upon spiritual resources to make peaceful progress through the wound, so to speak, towards the goal of healthier relationships, is the route this book will recommend.

Personal reversals can occur at any time in any place, of course – not only in the workplace while on the job. Inevitably, some personal reversals remain for a while and must be managed well if both person and career are to remain on track. Major reversals like illness, divorce, or the death of a dear one are not covered in this book, although the spiritual lifelines that are available here can be helpful in those cases as well.

There are ethical issues underlying most of the problems that surface throughout these pages. Having a functioning spirituality makes it a whole lot easier to 'do the right thing' when things get complicated or are otherwise going wrong in a workplace. You will have, I hope, after reading this book, a heightened ethical sensitivity, along with a deeper commitment to a functional spirituality.

Sadly, and all too often in the workplace today, decision makers, in the interest of efficiency and profits, are treating human beings like disposable parts. Whatever 'must be done' to reverse this unfortunate trend won't be done, I believe, without the support of a practical, faith-based spirituality.

ATTITUDES

Attitude is always important. A positive attitude tilts a positive person forward, into the wind, as it were. The positive tilt is a prerequisite for recovery from any setback. In the later chapters of this book, you'll learn about a rebound-and-recovery route, and find out how your spirituality can support and reinforce that positive attitude.

SPIRITUALITY IS EVERYWHERE – INCLUDING WHERE YOU WORK

The remarkable thing about the revival of faith-based spirituality in our day is that so much of it is taking place outside the churches.

This is not to say that organised religion, as such, is being dismissed as irrelevant by those who are searching for a meaningful spirituality. Some do dismiss it perhaps, but by no means all. There are good people, however, who are finding that religion, as they know it, is not helping them connect their faith commitments to secular concerns. The aim of this book is to try to close that gap, to encourage anyone willing to make his or her way through these pages to forge a meaningful connection between faith and work.

PART ONE

ON THE RELEVANCE OF
FAITH TO WORK AND LIFE

CHAPTER ONE
SPIRITUALITY AND THE HUMAN PREDICAMENT

WHAT IS SPIRITUALITY?

According to theologian Doris Donnelly, spirituality is prayer elevated to a lifestyle. That's one compelling definition of the reality that is prompting countless persons in these stressful times to stretch their souls towards God. Our undertakings are now 'soul size', as playwright Christopher Fry phrased it in *A Sleep of Prisoners*, and 'the enterprise is exploration into God'.

The question 'What is spirituality?' gives rise to another question: what are the roots of our current growing interest in spiritual issues?

More than sixty years ago in the US, *Time* magazine ran a cover story about an event that shook the world, an event that wounded many so profoundly that it has remained to trouble many of us, mind and soul, ever since. The incident, which was reported in the 20 August 1945 issue of the magazine, marked both an end and a beginning.

This report was published, as were all *Time* stories in those days, without attribution of authorship. I learned years later that a young (and then relatively unknown) *Time* staffer by the name of James Agee wrote the piece under a very tight deadline. The overarching headline was 'Victory'. The first subhead was 'The Peace'. The second subhead was 'The Bomb'.

Time was covering a big story that week, perhaps the biggest of the century. Agee saw the 'controlled splitting of the atom' that produced the bomb that was used to attack Hiroshima and Nagasaki, and thus bring to an end the greatest conflict in human history, as an event so enormous that, in comparison, 'the war itself shrank to minor significance'. To Agee's eye, '[H]umanity, already profoundly perplexed and disunified, was brought inescapably into a new age in which all thoughts and things were split – and far from controlled'.

Time's readers, still dizzy with the thrill of victory, could hardly have seen, as Agee did, the potential for both good and evil that the atomic bomb represented. That potential bordered 'on the infinite – with this further, terrible split in the fact: that upon a people already so nearly drowned in materialism even in peacetime, the good uses of this power might easily bring disaster as prodigious as the evil. ... When the bomb split open the universe ... it also revealed the oldest, simplest, commonest, most neglected and most important of facts: that each man is eternally and above all else responsible for his own soul, and in the terrible words of the Psalmist, that no man may deliver his brother, nor make agreement unto God for him.'

Then Agee made a shattering observation that rings every bit as true today as it did that memorable August many years ago. Here are the words he wrote – words that were available to any reader of America's most popular news magazine in 1945, and that have gone largely unheeded for more than six decades:

> Man's fate has forever been shaped between the hands of reason and spirit, now in collaboration, again in conflict. Now reason and spirit meet on final ground. If either or anything is to survive, they must find a way to create an indissoluble partnership.

These powerful words were perceptive and prophetic. They appeared just before the so-called 'baby boomers' were born. They explain the cause of the 'split' that has been troubling humanity for more than half a century. We have not yet forged the 'indissoluble partnership' between reason and spirit; we are even more adrift now than we were then on a sea of materialism. We may, however, be beginning to notice what Agee saw when the bomb split open the universe; namely, that each of us is responsible for his or her own soul.

Men and women in the world of work who are restless and wondering about the relevance of their Sunday faith to their

Monday responsibilities are, I believe, being nudged now by the Spirit, the Holy Spirit, to begin an exploration into God.

WHAT SPIRITUALITY ISN'T

'Spirituality' is not to be confused with the everyday sense of the word 'spirit' – as in 'school spirit', 'pioneer spirit', the 'spirit of capitalism', or the 'spirited' response someone might make to some external stimulus. To be *spirited* in such contexts is to react to something completely human, something finite. That which is truly *spiritual* is immaterial and cannot be fully grasped by our limited human minds; it cannot be measured, counted, weighed, or touched. It is seen only in its effects.

Spirit in a faith-based spirituality rooted in the Christian tradition is identified with the Holy Spirit, the Third Person of the triune God, present and active in the human soul. As scripture puts it: 'This is how we know that we remain in [God] and he in us, that he has given us his Spirit' (1 John 4:13).

In his Letter to the Galatians, Paul addresses people who are converts from paganism. He instructs them in the exercise of their new-found freedom in the Holy Spirit and urges them to 'live by the Spirit' in their normal secular surroundings. This is precisely what serious Christians at work in the world today are concerned about doing. How can one know that he or she is 'guided by the Spirit?'

THE PAULINE CRITERIA

Paul offers in Galatians 5:22-23 what I call the 'Pauline Criteria' for judging the consistency of one's own (or anyone else's) behaviour with the presence of the Spirit in a human life. They constitute what Paul calls the 'fruit of the Spirit'. There are nine and I listed them for you in the Introduction.

Examine what you do at home or in the workplace against these criteria. Judge another's oppositional or supportive behaviour in the light of these norms. These are non-market values that can humanise every marketplace and workplace.

Notice that Paul has not outlined unattainable goals. All nine of these Pauline characteristics are within your reach; they are attainable by normal people leading ordinary lives.

In contrast to these ingredients of a faith-based spirituality rooted in Christian revelation, Paul mentions the 'works of the flesh', i.e. human activity only, activity not informed by God's indwelling Spirit. The works of the flesh are what we are left with when we reject the Spirit and set out blindly on our own. These rebel elements are 'obvious', Paul notes, and he identifies them as follows: 'immorality, impurity, licentiousness, idolatry, sorcery, hatreds, rivalry, jealousy, outbursts of fury, acts of selfishness, dissensions, factions, occasions of envy, drinking bouts, orgies, and the like' (5:19-21). At the end of this catalogue, Paul puts it bluntly: 'I warn you, as I warned you before, that those who do such things will not inherit the kingdom of God.'

THE PRESENCE OF THE SPIRIT

After examining Paul's second list, you might be forgiven for thinking to yourself, 'Well, except for the orgies, that's actually a pretty fair description of the workplace as I know it'. That is all the more reason to focus closely on the first list of positive Pauline values.

If spirituality is to mean anything at all for you in the workplace, the Pauline Criteria signaling the presence of the Spirit must become the very infrastructure you carry with you into the world of work. They should be guiding principles, pillars that support your working life. Once internalised, they can serve as answers from within.

The Pauline Criteria can transform you, and with them you can transform the workplace. If you hope to change the world around you, change yourself!

Sober reflection on the absence in your surroundings (and perhaps even in yourself) of these positive criteria can be unsettling. So can the realisation of the occasional presence of what Paul listed as negatives. These experiences should be unsettling. Welcome the discomfort. It can serve an eviction notice on the complacency that can stifle the Spirit and the spirituality waiting to energise you from within your soul. Let's look now in detail at each of the nine Pauline values.

LOVE

The word means many things to many people. Popular culture debases love in song and story, forever confusing it with physical passion. Great literature and great lives through the centuries display the profound beauty of truly selfless love.

At bottom, love is service and sacrifice. It is the willingness to lay down one's life – literally or figuratively – for another. When you think about love, you should be thinking about your willingness to offer up your own true self for the benefit of another.

JOY

Joy is another profound reality that is not to be misunderstood. It is not to be confused with pleasure or hilarity. Those who replace the 'pursuit of happiness' with the pursuit of *pleasure* will find lasting joy always eluding them. Joy is an inner assurance that your will is aligned with God's will, that you are favoured, graced, and gifted beyond anything that you could merit on your own. Joy is balance, an abiding contentment.

PEACE

Often mistaken for whatever follows a truce, peace is actually tranquility.

St Thomas Aquinas described it as the 'tranquility of right order'. Those who 'bury the hatchet' and retain their grudges are not at peace. Those who retain their emotional balance and agree to disagree can live in harmony.

PATIENCE

This word literally means 'suffering'. The agent acts; the 'patient' receives the action.

How the person receives the action – especially the unwelcome action – is the test of patience. Tests of patience arise from countless sources: a dentist's drill; a honking horn; a fist pounding on the table; a spoken contradiction; an unmerited rebuke. The question is: how do you respond?

KINDNESS

Many have remarked that apparent kindnesses can, in fact, be acts of cruelty. This means that weakness or timidity can slip into virtue's clothing and provide cover for an escape from responsibility or right action. Many a selfish or hypocritical act has been justified by a bad motive that is wrapped in counterfeit kindness.

Kindness does not depend on the perceptions of others. True kindness is respect for human dignity in every circumstance of life; it is both courtesy and personally courageous attentiveness displayed towards another person.

GENEROSITY

The opposite of all that is small, closed, petty, ungiving, and unforgiving, generosity points to largeness of soul. Generosity does not come naturally to human nature. But generosity can be learned by observation and acquired by practice. Whenever practised, true generosity demonstrates the truth of the dictum that virtue is its own reward.

FAITHFULNESS

Dependability and reliability are the prerequisites of friendship. Keeping commitments – commonly thought of as 'promises' and theologically understood as 'covenants' – is the 'stuff' of faith.

For the believer, faith is the habit of entrusting oneself to God. In the workplace, faithfulness is friendship, trust, and the security derived from commitments kept. These two varieties of 'promises kept' may seem separate, but they actually reflect a single ongoing reality in the life of the believer.

GENTLENESS

Does being a 'gentle' man (or woman) imply refinement? withdrawal? a retiring personality? What does it mean to be gentle? Gentleness is so often confused with timidity that we are caught in a cultural confusion over the very meaning of the word and of the place of gentleness in the workplace. In actuality, gentleness is strength. The gentle person is neither insecure nor arrogant; he or she is self-possessed, in quiet control of self and the surrounding situation. Although meekness is sometimes praised in scripture ('Blessed are the meek ...'), it is too often dismissed as weakness. Because it is misunderstood, the quiet strength of true meekness is not given the fair chance it deserves to become a positive force in the workplace.

SELF-CONTROL
This test of personal integrity involves the practice of saying no to the self.

A young mother once held up her infant son in the presence of the legendary American Civil War general Robert E. Lee and asked for his blessing on the child. Lee offered an apt but rare and unusual blessing: 'Teach him he must deny himself', he said.

A person 'out of control' in matters large or small is a diminished person. To have 'lost it' in any circumstance of life is to have abdicated that which makes one human; it is to have invited a curse and rejected a blessing.

WELCOMING THE SPIRIT EVERY DAY – A PERSONAL CHECKLIST
Anyone seriously concerned with the challenge of changing workplace negatives into faith-based positives, or with welcoming the Spirit to dwell within his or her own soul, might well begin with Paul's nine-point checklist, making it an instrument of daily self-examination. Before your working day begins and at the end of the day before going to bed, compose yourself for a few stock-taking moments of prayer. You may want to use the following as a starting point for developing your own routine, but avoid the rote repetition of empty words and phrases. Be sure to allow for your own formulation of questions and selection of points for emphasis.

- ¬ Recall that you are in God's presence and thank God for the gift of life and any other gifts that come to mind.
- ¬ Ask for light to see yourself as God sees you, to see your day in the light of eternity.

Review your role in the day just unfolding, or just ending, against these norms:

LOVE
Morning: Am I prepared to share, serve, sacrifice for others today?
Evening: Did I open up towards others? Where did I hurt anyone or hold back?

JOY
Morning: Is my will aligned with God's? Do I cherish the graces, the gifts of God to me? Do I recognise the difference between pleasure and happiness? Am I in balance?
Evening: Where did I turn in on myself today? When and why did sadness touch me today? Did I lose balance?

PEACE
Morning: What image of tranquility can I carry with me into this new day?
Evening: Why was I upset? What grudges am I carrying? Did I disturb the peace of others? Did I make anyone angry?

PATIENCE
Morning: Am I prepared to suffer today, if God wills it or is willing to permit it?
Evening: When and why did I 'lose it' today? Did I overreact? Did I lose my temper because I was about to lose face? Do I really believe that everything depends on me?

KINDNESS
Morning: Am I prepared to be considerate today? Will courtesy and civility accompany me through the day, and will attentiveness mark my relationship to others?
Evening: Did I contribute any rudeness, abrupt demands, or insults to the rubble of this day?

GENEROSITY

Morning: What will I be today, a giver or a taker?
Evening: Was I petty, ungiving, or unforgiving in any way today? Did meanness enter the world today through me? Did I make anyone smile? Did I listen generously?

FAITHFULNESS

Morning: If God is God, he cannot be anything but faithful to me today and always. I resolve to remain faithful to God today and, with God's help, to keep all my commitments in faith and friendship, in dependability and reliability.
Evening: Was anyone let down by me today? Did I lose any faith in God or in myself? Did I violate any trusts?

GENTLENESS

Morning: I am capable of being rude, rough, and domineering. I want to be gentle. I hope the source of all gentleness will work through me today.
Evening: Was I harsh towards anyone today? Did I hurt anyone in any way?

SELF-CONTROL

Morning: I may have to say no to myself today; am I ready?
Evening: Did I leave any space for others today? Was I selfish or indulgent in ways that diminished the world's supply of human dignity?

Again, give thanks and, as needed, express not just regret but resolve to make amends.

Consider developing a daily sheet for monitoring your activity in each of the nine areas. Blank spaces on that sheet will allow you to monitor your own personal progress with regard to each of the Pauline values.

One item or another on the list of nine may call for special attention at a given stage in your life; you can highlight any category you like. You can also add other criteria that suit your purposes. Remember: the point of any exercise involving the Pauline Criteria is to heighten your awareness of God's presence in your life, and your responses to or rejections of God's promptings to you in the course of any day.

As you will discover later in this book, you are a vocation. You have been called by God. God never stops calling; that means you must never stop responding. Although the call is not vocalised in the familiar tones and patterns of speech that are part of your life, God's initiatives towards you are a no less essential part of your life. You simply have to learn to 'hear' these calls or 'read' them in the circumstances that surround you. After all, wherever you are, you are there by God's providence.

As a person with a calling, you must learn to listen for the specifics of that calling in the earthbound conversations of the secular settings where you are called to live the life God has given you.

If these Pauline Criteria for the presence of the Spirit in a human life are internalised – if they become part of who you are, regardless of where you are and what you do for a living – you will always carry them with you. Wherever you happen to be in work or life will become a better place for your presence there.

SPIRITUAL RESOURCES

Imagine that your spirituality provides you with a personal bank account to be drawn upon in troubled times. This is really not so wild a proposition. Have you noticed how often theological terms like 'providence' and 'trust' are used to name financial institutions?

The spiritual guidelines that the Pauline Criteria provide can function as deposit slips for the spiritual capital that is yours, by God's providence. You can always trust the God who knows you and calls you by name (no personal identification number needed) to maintain a positive balance in your account. You don't make the deposits; all you can do is have the good sense to make withdrawals as needed.

CONNECTIONS

So, here you are with a book in your hands and a desire, or at least a curiosity, to connect your religious faith to work and life.

The point of this chapter, and those that follow, is to help you act on that desire or that curiosity. The pages that follow will aim to enable you to deal productively not only with the wounds and reversals that are part of any life anywhere, but specifically with the challenges that are yours in the workplace. My aim is to help you do so in such a way as to make God present in this world, to make life better for others, to use your time in a manner that aligns your life with God's will for you.

The integration of religious faith and workplace responsibilities will bring balance to your life. And if you are called to a position of managerial or executive responsibility, you can create a workplace culture within which those you lead can themselves lead a balanced life.

I believe that you, as an individual, can overcome your personal share of the lethal 'split' between faith and reason, matter and spirit, that James Agee identified as a developing characteristic of the broader society. Once you do, your healing will move society one notch closer to the balance in these areas that it so conspicuously lacks. You will have done your part to create the 'indissoluble partnership' required to hold these fateful realities together as the human community struggles to maintain its sanity and live in hope on 'final ground'.

You will also, I believe, have unlocked for yourself the secret of a happy life in an imperfect world, a world that can deal with you at times harshly and unfairly.

GRADUAL PROGRESS

Much will depend on your willingness to let these spiritual truths sink into your soul as moisture seeps into the earth. It will not happen right away or all at once. Let these lines from Robert Frost's poem 'Snow' set the pace for the process of your personal assimilation of the wisdom principles that will keep you and your career on track in stressful times:

Our very life depends on everything's
Recurring till we answer from within.
The thousandth time may prove the charm.

Those answers 'from within', from the depths of a personal faith-based spirituality, are wisdom principles. They do not surface immediately when things go wrong. They have to push their way up through emotion, and ambition, and anger, and pride – through the negatives that will appear on your checkpoint screen during the recommended nightly review that I sketched out for you earlier. Developing a strong and functioning spirituality will take a while; the thousandth time may indeed prove the charm.

'IT'S A JUNGLE OUT THERE!'

You may now be thinking that the principles of spirituality outlined in this chapter will, if assimilated, arm you with little more than a simple slingshot when it comes to dealing with the unpredictable assaults you will face in your daily working life. Well, think about that for a moment. Recall that David did quite well against Goliath with that kind of equipment! Don't be too quick to discount or disregard the practical value of spirituality, a weapon that is both 'offensive' and 'defensive'.

And here is a point of capital importance for the hard-charging competitor who wants to succeed both in business and in the spiritual life: whenever you go on the offensive and activate your properly aggressive, competitive energies in the workplace, make sure that your style of assertiveness reflects the presence of the Pauline Criteria. Keep your competitiveness cool!

Spirituality is your *invisible* means of support, your ever-reliable resource in keeping yourself and your career on track when the going gets rough.

Perhaps your relationships with others in the workplace are going quite well at the moment. Perhaps you have no enemies;

it's simply not a 'jungle out there' for you. All is both serene and successful, so you may be wondering about the relevance for you right now of wisdom principles designed to sustain you when things go wrong.

And that, of course, is the point: things will go wrong eventually. It wasn't raining when Noah began to build his ark. The harmony and purpose in your workplace now should certainly be celebrated, but they probably shouldn't be relied on to endure forever.

In love and war, in spiritual and material combat, in religious and business ventures, fortune favours the well prepared. Even a minimal time investment in your personal spirituality will go a long way towards keeping you centred when events threaten, as they inevitably will, to pull you apart.

Your commitment to personal spirituality will also help you overcome complacency and reawaken courage from within. If you see yourself now as both serene and successful, consider this note of caution: you may not be feeling the tension; you may not yet experience any war in the workplace because you have not yet started to reject what is wrong in that 'jungle out there'. You may be too accommodating to your environment. 'No war' for you may mean that no spiritual growth is taking place.

AFFECT

I mentioned in the Introduction that management consultant and psychiatrist David E. Morrison sees a 'fit' for the Pauline Criteria in the workaday world. He sees people from a wide variety of workplaces. They come to him because they want to manage stress better; often their bosses want them to fit in better with functioning workplace teams. Morrison begins by focusing on a client's affect – an emotional state, the fundamental feeling that an individual expresses through eyes, voice, body language.

Since managing people means managing feelings, the people at Morrison Associates in Palatine, Illinois, USA (a suburb of Chicago), find themselves assisting clients who manage others by helping those clients identify and deal with feelings – the very feelings that are typically denied or ignored in the workplace. This is an area that is to be managed – not manipulated, but managed by us all.

There can be appropriate or inappropriate reactions to feelings in the workplace. Often, if you are willing to listen to them, your feelings can help you identify what is really going on.

A clarifying image employed by Morrison Associates to explain how feelings can impair thought is that of horse and jockey. The area of a human person where affect operates is like a horse; the area where thought works is like a jockey. Sometimes the horse gets out of control and throws the jockey. The affect can become too powerful not only for the one who possesses it at home or work, wherever the affected person happens to be, but also for those who are just observing or trying to understand the 'horse' in others.

In an interview, Dr Morrison explained to me that affect is the foundation upon which feelings, thought, and, eventually, behaviour rest. A stimulus will not gain your attention until it triggers an affect. If an individual has a persistent unmanageable affect, that person should see a health professional, says Dr Morrison. If an organisation has a persistent unmanageable affect, its leaders would probably be well advised to contact an organisation like Morrison Associates.

Following the lead of the late psychologist Silvan S. Tomkins, Morrison identifies nine affects. One is neutral, in that it affects all persons immediately and in much the same way; it is called 'Surprise-Startle'. Two are positive: 'Interest-Excitement' and 'Enjoyment-Joy'. Six are negative: 'Fear-Terror', 'Anger-Rage', 'Distress-Anguish', 'Shame-Humiliation', 'Disgust' and 'Contempt'. I see each of the hyphenated pairs as something of a 'one-two punch' or a 'two-stage rocket'. There is an amplifying force at work. Interest builds to excitement; enjoyment leads to joy; fear develops into terror, and so on. The stimulus triggers an affect that expands. Perhaps the most important point that David Morrison made when I mentioned the Pauline Criteria was that each and every one of them fits comfortably into the Enjoyment-Joy category; they lead to (i.e. amplify towards, extend into) a balanced self-possession, a kind of serene contentment at the centre of an active life. (Indeed, the Pauline value of joy is half of the descriptive label placed on this affect.)

The two positive affects – Interest-Excitement and Enjoyment-Joy – can be used to define a culture, says Morrison. Cultures, of course, are defined by dominant values. Interest-Excitement, he explains, describes a pervasive phenomenon in contemporary culture, as well as in the workplace. We live in settings of excessive hype and accelerated pace. We are over-amplified. The cultural thrust is towards excitement; but this excitement cannot be sustained.

Just consider, by way of example, the music, tone patterns, inflection, facial expressions, and staccato communication style characteristic of, say, five consecutive minutes of commercial television news delivery. Television provides a window on our stress-inducing world. We sit in front of that window on a daily basis and unconsciously adopt it as the backdrop for the daily drama (or, more accurately, daily melodrama) of the harried lives we create for ourselves.

Here is how Dr Morrison explained the two positive affects to me: 'If there is an optimal rise in the level of stimulation, you get Interest-Excitement. It starts off as interest and becomes excitement if the stimulation continues. This is a pleasant affect, so when someone finds the right level, he or she will move to it and seek to maintain it. This ranges from the interest of reading a book to the building excitement of sex.' He added that this affect can be a great motivator; it is one of the important reasons why we return to work each day. (A daily workplace routine that features no interest or excitement, of course, will rely solely on monetary or other inducements – not all of them pleasurable – to keep people coming back to work.)

Morrison explains Enjoyment-Joy this way: 'Imagine someone listening to a joke. That person is stimulated by the story. Often it is an odd or awkward situation being described; there is an element of discomfort. Tension builds and then suddenly, with the punch line, it stops. That's when there's laughter, i.e. enjoyment. When the uncomfortable stimulation, the suspension, stops, joy settles in. You see the same thing in people getting off a roller coaster. Enjoyment-Joy is there after the stress or distress is relieved and the need for comfort, for balance, has been met.'

The notion of contentment – a positive, abiding kind of balance – suggests itself to me as I think about this Enjoyment-Joy affect. I see it as serenity; you can be intensely active but your activity can be rooted in serenity. You have an anchor. You know where you stand. You know yourself.

This is the affect that is needed when people are hurting. However, Enjoyment-Joy is not, according to Morrison, fashionable in the contemporary workplace, where the dominant culture is Interest-Excitement. 'This Interest-Excitement pattern just doesn't do it for the human person', says Morrison. 'Think of the guy who drives up in a BMW and comes in here wearing designer clothes. He wants me to tell him how to manage his stress and put balance in his life. The Interest-Excitement culture tires you out.' In other words, the affect in place in many working people leaves them exhausted, rather than energised. So, it is up to the individual to consciously cultivate the Enjoyment-Joy affect. To ignore or minimise the importance of this task is, in my view, tantamount to ignoring or minimising your own proper role in preparing your soul for a better relationship with God.

WHERE WE COME FROM, WHERE WE ARE GOING
If you move about in the workaday world without giving any thought at all to your origins (from God) and your destiny (to be with God for all eternity), you are foolish indeed.

I hesitate to use the word 'fool', but anyone who ignores or denies a day-to-day dependency on God demonstrates impressive qualifications for full possession of that title. Psalm 14 offers the gentle reminder: 'Fools say in their hearts, There is no God'.

Human dependency upon a living, caring God is not passivity – just as serenity is not passivity. Nor does it point to the absence of freedom, for freedom and the ability to reason set us so-called rational animals apart from all other living beings. Moreover, to acknowledge this relationship of dependency is not, by that very fact, to declare yourself to be religious; it is simply to concede that you are not the sum and substance, let alone king or queen, of the universe. You may choose to accommodate yourself to this dependency without the help of church, synagogue, mosque, or shrine of any kind. You are free to make that choice. Such an accommodation would, however, still be an exercise of spirituality, the spirituality that is, as I mentioned, emerging now everywhere you look, outside the churches.

Religion and spirituality are distinct realities. Some good people view formal religion as an unappealing stained-glass abstraction far removed from the demands of daily living. As worthy of attention as such criticisms may be, it is difficult to comprehend how any good person can be *truly good* without some consciously forged spiritual links to the source of all goodness. These links may, as I say, be forged apart from any involvement with formal religion. In fact, commentators on religion, some to their dismay, some to their delight, are noticing that spirituality – the focus on ultimate origins, ultimate destinations, and the ultimate source of power and virtue – is not dead in contemporary life. It is simply happening as much or even more outside the churches, mosques, shrines, and synagogues as within them.

JOY
Think of the nine elements in the Pauline Criteria as stretching across the 'Enjoyment-Joy' spectrum that Dr Morrison employs. The goal, the term, the end, is a deep and lasting joy. That joy should reside deep within your soul – from enjoyment to joy.

The other positive affect, Interest-Excitement, would stretch you out towards ever higher levels of excitement, into a perpetual state of agitation. And that agitation would also be resident in your soul. There lies much of the discontent that troubles us today. It is already there in our mass-media culture; you don't have to make any effort to find it.

Beyond agitation, behind the ever-rising 'thresholds' of excitement and adrenaline, there is no such thing as a state of fulfillment. There is, however, enjoyment in what I commend to you as elements for the infrastructure of your spirituality. There is a positive, satisfying quality associated with each of Paul's nine points: love, joy, peace, patience, kindness, generosity, faithfulness, gentleness, and self-control.

Coming from within yourself, or seen in the effects of the actions of others, each of the Pauline elements has an expansive capacity. The expansion or enlargement moves you towards balance; it leads the soul towards security. How well you know the way events can whirl around you; that will surely continue. You also know how activity can catch you up; that will not change. But what you may not yet know is the capacity of this spirituality to keep you rooted in joy (because it roots you in God) while setting you free for the full human pursuit of all good things.

LIMITATION

One good image that catches the tension between human freedom and dependency under God, while providing a window of sorts on what I like to call the human predicament, is that of a puppet on a string.

Of course, the human person under God is more than a puppet. And God, while certainly not a puppeteer, has to be understood as more than a mere observer of human activity. Events are not all random and out of divine control; human beings are not completely autonomous and fully in charge of their own destinies.

Thoughtful believers acknowledge God to be all-powerful and they celebrate the fact that God endows every human person with freedom to act and choose as he or she pleases – wisely or foolishly. The reflective person of faith is left, however, with the theological problem of figuring out the relationship between divine fore-knowledge and human freedom.

Human freedom is part and parcel of the human predicament. You are a contingent being who is free to choose. Your choices can result in gain or loss, life or death. And no matter how wisely and well you choose, limits surround you at every turn. The ending of life as you know it is always a possibility, usually regarded as remote, but undeniably inevitable.

History offers perspective on the human predicament, on the contingent state of being that is yours by virtue of your being human. Two hundred years ago this world was filled with human beings. Not one of them is alive today. Two hundred years from now, no one now on earth will still be alive. Two hundred years is a very, very short time in the long view of history. Cut that span of years by one hundred and you face the same conclusion: your journey through life is short.

Yet, caught as you are in the human predicament, you kick against limits, struggle to achieve, and act as if you hold permanent title or a perpetual lease on life, health, and possessions. Simply put, the human predicament is the inseparability of growth and decline in the unrepeatable onceness of a human life.

LIVING AND DYING
It has been remarked that people may or may not believe in God, but they all believe in death and do all they can to defer it.

There is just no escaping it. You start to die when you begin to live. You move towards the end the moment you set out on the journey. Everything in you reaches up, even as the gravitational pull of human limitations holds you down. At various stages of your life, that down-pulling weight is so light you hardly notice it; you can easily forget it is there. But it always is.

At many milestones on your journey, the absolute endpoint is remote and far from view, and you fail to notice it. Your attention is fixed on nearer-term goals that take on dimensions of importance and permanence, labels that are laughable when you experience the shock of recognising them in their relationship to your ultimate goal and purpose in life.

This recognition is the by-product of a functioning spirituality, which, as I noted at the outset, is a by-product of prayer. Busy people have to be encouraged to 'waste' more time with God in prayer. Trapped in the human predicament, believers typically turn to God with prayers of petition, in search of a 'fix' when things go wrong. They rarely associate their musings, ponderings, and puzzlings over their relationship to a higher power with the act or practice of prayer. Those mental meanderings happen, however, in moments that most people cherish: time spent walking along the shore, staring into a fireplace, looking at the stars, gazing at the mountains, listening to a symphony, watching a baby crawl. Those reflective moments can, of course, happen in a cathedral or a subway station, in sacred space intended to be conducive to prayer, or in ordinary, walk-around, lunch-hour surroundings. Those reflective moments will, if you let them, occur.

Whether it is human architecture or natural beauty that provides the setting, the believer needs to find the space and time for permitting God to become more fully present to his or her own consciousness, more fully resident within his or her own heart. Once you do this, and take the next step of letting the effects of this consciousness rise to manifest themselves in your attitudes and external behaviour, you have a functioning spirituality.

Prayer of petition, not at all to be denigrated or disregarded, can be a proving ground for the higher level of meditative communication with God. Caught in any one of a million predicaments that go along with the human condition, believers will typically and spontaneously beg for assistance. 'God help me' is more than an idle phrase useful for providing punch to a narrative. 'Please, God, let …' 'Dear Lord, help …' 'O, God, don't …' The point to notice when you make a prayer of petition is that your prayer is like the rope thrown from a boat to the dock when you are ready to come ashore. You catch the rope on a cleat, not to pull the dock to you, but to pull yourself towards the dock.

The point of your prayer of petition should be to line up your will with God's, so that you can be 'pulled' by grace towards God to accept whatever it is that God regards as best for you. Not my will but 'thy will be done' is the qualifier that should accompany any request for divine help. If you understand this, you will have opened up your soul for a fuller stretch towards the God who cannot be anything but faithful to you, and who will be there for you in any wound, reversal, or recovery that you experience as you work your way through the human predicament.

For the intellectual, the human predicament is the troublesome split between science and religion, or more broadly, between faith and reason. For the artist, it is the split between mind and heart. For the ordinary person trying to figure things out, it is the tension between the conscious experience of being personally affected by growth and decline, and the often unconscious anxiety associated with a personal, sometimes lonely journey that stretches from birth to death, in an environment of risk, on an unfamiliar road called life.

With the nine Pauline Criteria as guideposts for the journey, you can move ahead with confidence and courage to meet the challenges that lie ahead.

CHAPTER TWO
MIXING FAITH AND WORK

It may be hard for you to believe that what happened to John Koepke ever happened. It will probably be even more difficult for you to believe that it could happen to you. But it did happen to John; and it could happen to you. If it ever does happen to you, you may find yourself wondering about the relationship of faith to work; you may, in fact, find yourself searching for a spirituality to help you cope.

John was president and chief operating officer of a small graphics company. He reported directly to a working chairman. Just before he was ready to leave home for work one morning, John's wife Pat passed along some bad news she had received just the day before: she had breast cancer.

John was stunned, saddened, and understandably upset. He wanted to stay with Pat that day, but it was simply impossible. An important meeting was scheduled with people coming in from out of town; he absolutely had to attend.

When he arrived at work, the chairman saw that something was wrong and said, 'John, you look upset. What's the problem?'

'I just got some bad news', John replied. 'Pat told me this morning that she learned yesterday she has breast cancer.'

'Well, John,' the chairman pronounced, 'maybe you ought to get all your bad news on the same day. I'm afraid I've got to let you go.'

John was reeling – for the second time within only a few hours. Although he had received a handsome raise just weeks before, he decided not to fight the dismissal. He later told me that he realised he had been trapped for some time in a dysfunctional situation. Best to break away promptly, he thought, and get home to take care of his wife. As if he needed further proof that he was working for a crazy outfit, John soon learned that his contractually-assured twelve-month severance period had been unilaterally cut to six, and the 100 per cent of compensation that was to continue for a year in the event of involuntary separation had been unilaterally cut in half.

After reviewing all the options, John decided not to litigate, choosing instead to get on with his life and help Pat get on with hers.

Both, by the way, are now doing fine. John is running his own company and Pat is in remission. 'We were the best of friends when we got married,' John told me (in Pat's presence), 'and having been through all this together, we're better friends today.'

VOCATION

Ed Willock, editor of the long-defunct magazine *Integrity*, composed the following verse around the end of World War II, as the great American business machine was returning to the task of meeting peacetime economic needs:

Mr Business went to church,
He never missed a Sunday;
But Mr Business went to hell
For what he did on Monday.

That dart may have been amusing back then, but, despite horror stories that John Koepke and many others can still tell, it is wide of the mark now as the sense of a vocation to business is on the rise. The notion that work is somehow set apart, compartmentalised from one's spirituality, is one that most working people find unacceptable. This raises the question: why are you there, wherever you show up for work on Monday, in the first place?

This is a question of vocation. What is your calling? Everyone has one. What is yours? And if you have a vocation to business, how can you treat your associates in the workplace with anything less than dignity and respect, knowing that God called both you and them to be there?

As a youngster growing up in Philadelphia, Pennsylvania, I frequently heard the word 'vocation', but it was typically used in only one of two ways. The first was in reference to a 'vocational school' where students uninterested in or unqualified for enrollment elsewhere on an 'academic track' took carpentry, printing, or other 'vocational' courses. The second sense referred to some form of religious ministry.

I learned that, in a religious context, Protestant ministers were 'called' to serve a particular congregation, and that young Catholics were urged to consider a 'vocation' to priesthood or religious life. Both situations represented something special that was given by God; the 'call' was not to be taken lightly. If accepted, a vocation was, in the pious imagination, carried around much like a piece of air-travel luggage that could be 'lost' at almost any point on the journey. Anyone who refused or lost this 'higher calling' was thought to be running no small degree of personal, spiritual risk.

This use of the vocabulary has fallen out of fashion nowadays. Young people are encouraged to think not in terms of 'having' or 'losing' a vocation, but of being a vocation. The theologically correct approach to this issue is reflected in a very direct statement of identity: you *are* a vocation.

You are, in other words, responding to a call from the God who formed you in your mother's womb, called you then, and never stops calling. It is not as if God placed a call to you, left a message in your voice mail, and then hung up. On the contrary, you are being called, person-to-person, at every moment of your life. Do not, however, expect to hear a voice in this communication. You will hear this call in the circumstances of your life, in the people who nurture or disappoint you, in the opportunities or frustrations that present themselves, in your temperament and talents, in your physical and intellectual capacities, and in your aspirations and desires.

All of these are gifts to you from God. Faith instructs you to use them according to God's will for your salvation, for his glory, and for the service of your fellow human beings. That is what you are 'called' by God to be and to do. And because

God calls you to do it, the work – whatever form it takes – has inherent dignity.

Martin Luther King once said, 'If a man is called to be a street sweeper, he should sweep streets even as Michelangelo painted, or Beethoven composed music, or Shakespeare wrote poetry. He should sweep streets so well that all the hosts of heaven and earth will pause to say, here lives a great street sweeper who did his job well.'

ANSWERING GOD'S CALL

There is, I want to emphasise, a genuine vocation to business and to the daily working life. Men and women are called by God to serve one another in the context of buying and selling, producing and consuming, supplying and demanding the material goods and services that sustain and enrich human life. The fact that financial benefit arises from a transaction is hardly evidence that God is absent from the lives of those conducting the transaction.

There are, of course, many other 'callings' anyone might consider. The trick is to determine which call is for you. This determination requires prayer.

You must choose in freedom the place and the occupation where your prayer suggests that God is calling you to be. You'll never know for certain, but faith has a way of convincing you that you are where God wants you to be. If you feel otherwise, that in itself may be a message to move on. The point to bear in mind, however, is that you are not a random fluctuation in some complex system of occupational distribution. You are a person who is known and cherished by a creator-God who has something special for you in mind. Even if prayer was the farthest thing from your mind when you prepared yourself for a particular way of life – taking this job or that, selecting one profession over another, living here or there – God was not disinterested or disengaged from the process. God's providence was there at least permitting and perhaps promoting the outcome of your unreflective choices. Regardless of the presence or absence of prayerful reflection on your part as you moved through life to where you are at this present moment, you can decide now to begin listening more attentively to the God who calls; you can attempt to read more carefully the will of God in the circumstances where you find yourself right now. You are a vocation.

PURPOSEFUL VOCATION

I've always liked the following reflection-prayer of John Henry Cardinal Newman. It is one of the ponderables that belongs in any workplace spirituality. It is an assertion of purpose and vocation even when you are tempted to believe that your compass is gone and your life is devoid of meaning:

> I am created to do something or to be something for which no one else is created; I have a place in God's counsels, in God's world, which no one else has; whether I be rich or poor, despised or esteemed by man, God knows me and calls me by my name.

> God has created me to do him some definite service; He has committed some work to me which he has not committed to another. I have my mission – I may never know it in this life, but I shall be told it in the next. Somehow I am necessary for his purposes. ...

> I am a link in a chain, a bond of connection between persons. He has not created me for nothing. I shall do good; I shall do His work. I shall be an angel of peace, a preacher of truth in my own place while not intending it – if I do but keep His commandments.

> Therefore, I will trust Him, whatever, wherever, I am, I can never be thrown away. If I am in sickness, my sickness may serve Him; in perplexity, my perplexity may serve Him; if I am in sorrow, my sorrow may serve Him. He does nothing in vain ... He knows what He is about. He may take away my friends, He may throw me among strangers, He may make me feel desolate, make my spirits sink, hide my future from

me – still He knows what He is about. (*Meditations and Devotions*, 'Hope in God – Creator', 7 March 1848)

It may be true that week after week, for most of the weeks of their working lives, millions of Christians who worship on Sunday move back into the Monday world of business (or any other workplace setting) without giving much thought to the relevance of their religious faith to business practice. But it is also true that theological reflection, practical pastoral advice, and a renewed interest in spirituality are encouraging committed Christians to integrate their religious commitments with their business responsibilities for a unified grace-filled life. The resulting spiritual benefits are all the more important when the walls of the workplace begin to close in and stifle the spirit of the person employed there; or worse, when accumulated stress causes those walls to start tumbling down, crushing the human spirit.

A friend of mine once remarked, 'If you feel called to what you are doing, and if you really like what you do, you'll never work a day in your life!' The integration of faith and work can make that joyful conclusion possible. When linked to faith, a working life becomes a life that is really worth living!

'WHAT IS THE PURPOSE OF BUSINESS?'
All that has gone before in this book by way of reflection on workplace spirituality will help you come up with your own answer to the question of what it means for you to be a Christian in a secular workplace setting, Monday to Friday, nine to five. Are the Pauline Criteria – the nine spiritual principles, the nine supportive pillars – in evidence there? Are they present as a result of *your presence* – not your preaching, mind you, but your presence? Are they instinctive to you?

These are all fundamental questions that lead to another fundamental question: what is the purpose of business?

'To maximise profits' is no answer; to 'optimise' profits is not particularly helpful, either. Neither explains the deeper purpose of business activity. Nor is it fully satisfying to couch the 'purpose' of business in terms of maximising the long-term viability of the firm.

Business, I would argue, deals essentially with exchanges. If you are in business as owner, manager, or worker somewhere down the line, you are doing for others on condition of receipt of something of fair value in return.

Persons in business relate to other persons whose needs, preferences, and desires are met, to some degree of satisfaction, by the product or service the business is organised to provide – at a price. To meet that need, preference, or desire is the purpose of business. To do so at a price (and thus differentiate the activity from voluntarism or altruism) means receiving in exchange sufficient remuneration to cover, at the very least, the costs (including risk) of providing the service or product. This enables the provider to receive the income necessary to meet his or her own legitimate needs, preferences and desires. Otherwise, the business system, the network of relationships where need and satisfaction meet as question and answer, could not attract and hold you the provider; you would have to find some other way to 'make a living'.

Why you choose business to occupy your reimbursable time, instead of earning income in another of the many ways open to you, is a good question. Could it be that you chose business because you were, in fact, chosen for this way of life, called to it? This points to the possibility of business as your calling, your vocation; it suggests that business has a special place in the divine plan for you.

The business organisation is there to meet, on the buyer's side, a human need for product or service. For the seller, business generates necessary income. The business context, with all its market intermediaries, enables the needs of both buyer and seller to be met in a reliable, predictable, organised fashion. Such a system, of course, makes it possible for people in our society, and societies like ours, to get on with the daily dynamic of life.

Business organises the material basis for human existence and well-being. Business is thus seen as foundational to the construction of a community's material relationships; and not material only. There is also a range of social, cultural and personal goods that business brings to the construction of a good society.

If you are in business, you should take proper credit for the fact that you are fostering a human good that would not be achieved without you and the others who form the business community.

Your purpose for being in business is rooted in a great deal more than simply making money. Sure, just as food is necessary for life, profit is necessary for the life and health of a business. No argument about that. But who would recommend that you maximise your intake – stuff yourself full – of food at every opportunity?

If you are a leader in business (or any other kind of organisational life), your purpose is to help create a culture within which your associates can lead a balanced life. You have an opportunity to make life (quite literally) richer for others, to do something here on earth that makes this world receptive for a kingdom that is coming, a promised kingdom of justice and peace.

NEEDS, PREFERENCES, DESIRES

Need, preference, and desire are graded considerations in the provision of goods and services by organised business activity.

If, for example, you are organised to make available essential food, shelter, clothing, education, medicine, security, and healthcare, you are in the business of meeting basic needs. If your business is directed towards meeting preferences, as opposed to needs, your product or service will go beyond the essentials and move from a focus on *vivere* to *bene vivere*, from survival to comfort. Consumer preference invites the supplier to move towards the fancy, but not the frivolous product offering.

If desire only is active on the demand side, you are probably operating in a luxury marketplace. Of course, what is viewed as necessity at the high end of the market, may be luxury to the eyes of consumers at the lower end.

In your estimate of all this, if you grant priority to need over both preference and desire, you might say that provision to meet material human need is the immediate and fundamental purpose of business. All the same, meeting preferences, not basic needs, accounts for most of the volume of business activity and is, of course, in most settings, a worthy purpose.

Most human desires are healthy, wholesome and normal – but not all of them. When business aims to satisfy unreasonable and even harmful desire, or worse, promotes and stimulates personally and socially harmful desire, the purpose of business is perverted. If you are carrying a faith-based spirituality with you into the workplace, you will surely find yourself becoming more sensitive not only to what that workplace is doing to those employed there, but also to what impact that organisation's product or service is having, for good or for ill, on its clients and customers. If the place or the product is hurting people, you have a choice: change things or get out, otherwise you shrink into a person of diminished integrity if you remain in that job. Each believer will have to make his or her own choices on this score, but certainly any commitment to a career based on increasing the sales of harmful or addictive consumer products, say, or pornography (to offer an obvious example), needs re-examining in light of the nine Pauline values.

Unreasonable desire can be at work on the supply side of the exchange too. Where greed, far removed from need or legitimate preference, drives the income motivation of the provider – the seller – the business mechanism is abused for unreasonable personal gain. Society is not only ill-served but seriously injured by abuses on either side of the exchange. If you notice this happening in or around your organisation, that will surely motivate you to change it if you can. If change is not a realistic option, your discomfort with a greed-based corporate culture should be enough to send you packing.

EMPLOYMENT ... AND GOD'S ACTION
Another purpose of business is to provide employment – an organised environment within which individuals can come together, on a regular and stable basis, to provide service to others and earn income for personal and family support.

It would be difficult to exaggerate the value to society of providing economic security to working persons and those who depend on them. We look to business to do just that, although few today expect any single business organisation to provide uninterrupted employment for all its workers all their working lives.

From a theological perspective, business can be seen as relating in a privileged way to the Creator. From the very beginning, all creation is God's action. All created things depend on God and God's continuing activity. This critically important point was emphasised – not just for Catholics, but for the whole world – by the Second Vatican Council:

> For without the Creator the creature would disappear. For their part, however, all believers of whatever religion have always heard His revealing voice in the discourse of creatures. But when God is forgotten the creature itself grows unintelligible. (*Pastoral Constitution on the Church in the Modern World*, no. 36).

All of us have the opportunity to participate, through our human work, in the ongoing activity of the Creator. Those who work in business can hear God's revealing voice 'in the discourse of creatures', no matter how earthbound and material that discourse may be.

RELATIONSHIPS IN BUSINESS

All of business activity is relational, and the relationship is dual: (1) to God the Creator of that which is transacted or exchanged, and (2) to those who engage in the variety of transactions that constitute business activity. The first relationship is really worship (an obvious opportunity for Sunday to spill over into Monday); the second is, in fact, a vocation – the call to work with others in advancing God's creative activity.

This opens up yet another theological perspective. Men and women in business are not, strictly speaking, creators, but they are stewards. Stewardship is a human responsibility and the business environment is an ideal setting within which to meet that responsibility.

Your spirituality will acknowledge that the idea of stewardship is rooted in the first verse of the 24th Psalm: 'The earth is the Lord's, and the fullness thereof'. The 'earth' – meaning all of material creation – belongs to God. So does the 'fullness thereof': the fruit, the yield, the extract, the product, the construct, the artifact, or whatever emerges as the formed, forged, or finished result of human interaction with the resources of 'the earth'. All of it belongs to the Lord. The human person is the manager, the steward.

Our legal conventions assign and protect our 'ownership' rights, but in the theological perspective ownership rights are, in fact, stewardship responsibilities. What we own is the Lord's. What we do through human work is done by the Lord at work within us. This perspective supplies a solid theological foundation for the release of your human potential in full-time business activity.

Business provides the context for human interaction in pursuit of all the worthy purposes mentioned above; it also comes as close as anything I can imagine to the definition of stewardship.

There is theological significance in your human action of making available, through fair exchanges, the goods and services people need, prefer, and in some cases simply desire. There is also theological meaning in your managerial and entrepreneurial function of making employment available for others – helping them to be more active and productive human beings.

UNION WITH GOD, UNION WITH OTHERS

Your ultimate purpose, theologically speaking, is union with God and others in the human community. Your journey begins with God and, make no mistake, is intended to end with God at the conclusion of an experience of sin and grace, and the gift of redemption through a covenant community called church. Your journey is, of course, in, and of, and through a material world that theology sees as 'good'. The purpose of your business activity, in a theological perspective, is to serve a people on the way to salvation by organising the material and social basis of their transit through life. This is something to think about any day on your way to work, and any time you hear yourself praying, 'Thy kingdom come'! The Kingdom is indeed coming, and what you are doing Monday to Friday, nine to five, is intended in God's great plan for the world to be part of that reality!

On Sundays, those Christians who emphasise the sacramental life are conscious of themselves as communicants, bread-breakers. They remember their Lord in the breaking of the bread. Rarely do they reflect on the etymological link between the companies that employ them on weekdays and the Eucharist they celebrate on Sundays. The Latin phrase *cum pane* ('with bread') describes their Sunday 'com-panionship'. The companies to which those called to business return, refreshed and rested, on Monday mornings can be infused by them with a spirit of cooperation and, yes, genuine companionship.

In families, there is association by kinship. In faith communities, there is association by conviction. In corporations (even those that call themselves 'families'), kinship is not what holds persons together. But conviction could work that way, particularly the kind of conviction that stems from a deeper religious faith.

Business firms, then, are organised to serve the material needs of the human community, and working there can easily be viewed as 'just a job'. But it can also be seen, with the eye of faith, as a vocation to work not only in companies, but also in companionship. It can be viewed as service not simply to clients or customers, but to persons destined, like you, for eternal life. This perspective moves the believer beneath the bottom line to an appreciation of the relevance of religious faith to business practice. It stretches Sunday into Monday, and beyond. It suggests that retirement benefits for the 'faithful steward' (see Luke 12:42) are quite literally out of this world.

That is something worth thinking about right now and incorporating into the 'whole nine yards' of the Pauline Criteria that run through this book. Love, joy, peace, patience, kindness, generosity, faithfulness, gentleness, and self-control belong in the business environment – to humanise it, sanctify it, restore it to emotional balance, and render it truly efficient and effective for the long haul. That is the silent but compelling statement you make when you carry them with you as you go to work on Monday morning.

Recall my suggestion to view these nine spiritual guidelines as spanning Morrison's Enjoyment-Joy category, i.e. as expanding from the initial affect of enjoyment to a deeper sense of abiding joy. Enjoyment engages you with your work; continued application of your talents to the task can lead to genuine joy, a deep joy within your soul. That, in my view, is the meaning of those words all of us wish we could say all the time, 'I really love my work'.

Love it or leave it, I would add. If there is no room in your workplace for the first of the nine criteria, how can you believe that God really wants you to be there? It may not be realistic to expect your work always to be pleasurable, but it should be joyful with that deep-down joy of knowing that it is a place where you can find God, and where God wants you to be. It is possible, of course, to be 'stuck', by God's permissive will, in work you simply cannot love. You can't get out. Read on and you will see how the spiritual guidelines traced out in these pages can become sustaining lifelines for you in dealing with such situations.

CHAPTER THREE
PREPARING FOR ADVERSITY IN LIFE AND WORK

Not long ago, an out-of-work executive called me for advice. His job search was going nowhere. His divorce had just been finalised. His battle for weekly visitation rights to his only son was bogged down in red tape and made all the more painful because his son didn't really care about seeing him.

This man told me that he wanted to develop a deeper sense of spirituality in his life. He had become convinced, he said, that 'organised religion is for people who are afraid of going to hell, but spirituality is for those who have already been there'. He is a very good and decent person. Why, he wanted to know, were all the negatives piling up on him?

BAD TIDINGS
Rabbi Harold S. Kushner's wise, warm, and wonderful book, *When Bad Things Happen to Good People* (Schocken Books, 1981), addresses just such difficult questions. It is written from the heart of a deeply religious man who has himself encountered great adversity in life. Kushner's son Aaron was diagnosed in infancy as having a condition called progeria, 'rapid aging'. The rabbi learned that his son would never grow much beyond three feet tall or have any hair on his head or body. The boy would have the appearance of a little old man. And he would die in his early teen years.

Rabbi Kushner spoke of his son in the Introduction to the volume. 'This is his book,' Kushner wrote, 'because any attempt to make sense of the world's pain and evil will be judged a success or failure based on whether it offers an acceptable explanation of why he and we had to undergo what we did.' Two of Kushner's chapter titles reflect questions that are part

of the human predicament: 'Why Do the Righteous Suffer?';
'What Good, Then, is Religion?'

These questions are on the minds of most thinking people
in the face of human tragedy, and remain unexpressed by
many. It is important for one's spiritual and mental health not
only to bring these and similar questions to the forefront of
consciousness, but to talk them over with trusted friends. It
is also important to recognise that these questions can be
answered only in the vocabulary of spirituality, as indeed Rabbi
Kushner demonstrates towards the end of his book:

> Let me suggest that the bad things that happen to us in our
> lives do not have a meaning when they happen to us. They
> do not happen for any good reason which would cause us to
> accept them willingly. But we can give them a meaning. We
> can redeem these tragedies from senselessness by imposing
> meaning on them. The question we should be asking is not,
> 'Why did this happen to me? What did I do to deserve this?'
> That is really an unanswerable, pointless question. A better
> question would be, 'Now that this has happened to me,
> what am I going to do about it?' (p. 136)

As I read those words, I wondered what meaning a Christian
spirituality – as Christian – might impose on them. Is there a
Christian perspective, I asked, that might enlarge the interpretative framework needed to figure these things out and decisively
respond to the what-am-I-going-to-do-about-it question?

MEANING

From my Christian point of view, I wondered whether some
'bad things' might not 'have a meaning' when they happen.
(The crucifixion of Jesus comes to mind.) Such events could
indeed, I found myself thinking, be accepted willingly for a very
good theological reason. There is, of course, an unacceptable
reason that I would dismiss along with Rabbi Kushner; namely,
that something someone did makes him or her 'deserve' this
truly horrific outcome. That kind of thinking turns God into

some kind of mean-spirited umpire anxious to call you 'out' at the plate, instead of waiting, like the father of the prodigal son in Luke's Gospel parable, to welcome you home.

Both Jewish and Christian spirituality are careful not to put the blame on God when reversals occur. So-called 'acts of God' are really acts of nature. It is true, of course, that God is the creator of all things natural, but nature's laws – the law of gravity, for example – play themselves out without divine interference. Kushner is particularly good on this point, refusing to blame God for the agony of a particular cancer patient, but insisting at the same time that the action of God is clearly visible in the 'gifts' bestowed on such patients: 'The strength to take each day as it comes, to be grateful for a day full of sunshine or one in which they are relatively free of pain.'

According to Kushner, the vexing questions that enter the lives of those who find the world closing in on them – the victims of disease or downsizing, the survivors who mourn the death of a spouse or child – will surface in every life and recur in every generation. 'The questions never change,' he observes; 'the search for a satisfying answer continues.' That is where I found myself pausing as I read this insightful book – a book I readily recommend to anyone burdened with tragedy and distress – and coming to a different conclusion, one that I had the opportunity to mention to Rabbi Kushner in a conversation we had some years ago.

SEPARATE CONCLUSIONS

For me, and for those who believe as I do, the search has ended in Christ. This is not to say that I, or we, or anyone else 'has all the answers'. I mean only to say that the reflective Christian has met Christ as a serious questioner meets a satisfying answer. Christian spirituality savours the satisfaction of the answer in a challenging, but never complacent way. The challenge is what Christians call the Paschal Mystery, an intriguing notion to be explored below.

Any person of faith, Jew or Christian, can agree with Kushner's observation that the success in your search for answers depends a lot on what you mean by 'answer'. If you expect fully satisfying explanations, there is 'probably no satisfying answer'. The pain 'will still be there'.

But so will you still be there. And life will be there challenging you to get on with it, to face up to the future, to help others, to love and smile and grow, and to believe that God is there with you, right there at your side. 'That's the spirit', you might find yourself saying to someone else who is trying in this way to rebound bravely and recover from a shattering reversal. The 'spirit' you admire is, in fact, a functioning spirituality; it is evidence of the presence of the Holy Spirit in the human soul.

SOFT SOLUTIONS TO HARD PROBLEMS

The spirituality that underlies this book equips you with some admittedly soft solutions to life's hard problems. As I mentioned earlier, this book provides you with invisible means of support. You may try it out, as Peter tried walking on the water (Matthew 14:28-31), only to lose heart and start to sink. Or you may stick with it and adopt the spiritual solutions contained in these pages as forces that imperceptibly supply balance, coherence, and consistency to all you do.

Peter's problem related to shaky faith. He and a boat full of disciples of Jesus were quite a distance from shore on a windy night in very choppy waters. Matthew's Gospel (14:28-31) recounts that Jesus 'came toward them walking on the sea'. When the disciples saw him walking on the water they were terrified, but Jesus said to them, 'Take courage, it is I; do not be afraid'. He then invited Peter to come towards him – to walk on the waves. As the gospel account tells it, 'Peter got out of the boat and began to walk on the water toward Jesus'. For the moment, Peter's faith sustained him. But when he saw how strong the wind and the waves were, he faltered, began to sink, and cried for help. And the gospel account, in words that have found their way into the hearts of countless Christians, says: 'Immediately Jesus stretched out his hand and caught him, and said to him, "O you of little faith, why did you doubt?"'

Belief in Jesus as Son of God and the Messiah sets Christians apart from Jews; it is a fundamental difference between the faiths. And the difference lies not simply in an assent, on the part of Christians, to the proposition that Jesus is divine. It is more complex than that. The difference works itself out in a spirituality that integrates, however incompletely, the dimensions of the so-called Paschal Mystery.

This expression encompasses the reality of Easter – the sufferings, death, resurrection and ascension of Jesus. The Paschal Mystery enables the eye of Christian faith to 'see' that there is life through death, a notion that is rooted in the Hebrew scriptures that relate the story of the original 'pasch' or 'passover'. The Paschal Mystery provides an interpretative framework wherein the Christian comes to believe that the route to glory passes through shame and humiliation. In this faith-based value system, loss is the price of gain; defeat is the preface to victory. For those who believe this, personal hardships – including those encountered on the job – do in fact have meaning, and transcendent meaning at that.

This specifically Christian perspective raises a host of intriguing issues. For example, in his book *Why Work* (Simon and Schuster, 1988), Michael Maccoby plays on Lord Acton's famous saying, 'Power tends to corrupt, and absolute power tends to corrupt absolutely'. Maccoby offers as a corollary to Acton's dictum, 'the equally certain law that powerlessness perverts' (p. 67). Christians, however, have a basis in faith for not overlooking the power of powerlessness.

Dealing with workplace difficulties can be a spiritual exercise, one that adds meaning to life and work. Just as the Father raised Jesus from the dead, the Christian's Easter faith would maintain, so those whose baptism 'plunged' them sacramentally and symbolically into the death of Jesus will also rise with Jesus for eternal glory. The process begins with baptism, which enables the baptised symbolically to 'die' with Jesus and then 'rise' to walk in 'newness of life' (the life of grace). In that 'death' is to be found a faith-based reality that puts the sorrows and setbacks of life into proper perspective, where they can be seen as preludes to glory.

Belief in the resurrection of Jesus is central to the Christian faith. To try to figure out exactly how that event happened is to reduce a mystery to a problem to be solved. The only 'solution' is faith, the faith that enables Christians to make sense out of pain, suffering, illness, disappointment, defeat, and death. They know, by faith, that 'resurrection' recoveries are available to them, by God's grace, in the aftermath of any reversal on their journey through life. They eventually die knowing that, again by God's grace, they will rise from death to eternal life.

AMAZING, INDEED

Knowing all this by faith, Christians find themselves at Easter time singing 'Amazing Grace' and giving thanks to God in Christ for making their redemption possible. If all this is true, they find themselves thinking that this life, with all its difficulties, is something tremendously worth living to the full. Sure it has its ups and downs, but all of it – pain and gain, sorrow and joy, defeat and victory – is good precisely because God chose to make it so in Christ.

So, when bad things happen to good Christians, they are able to call upon their own interpretative framework to search for a deeper meaning, a meaning that is available only to the eye of faith. This is not a grin-and-bear-it exercise, or a matter of 'carrying your cross'. The meaning I am pointing to derives from a quiet conviction that the glorified Jesus, the victorious Jesus, lives now in glory. He is an eternal 'winner' who is at the side of every believer at every stage of the believer's life. Christ's victory, in short, can never be reversed. And therein lies the basis for the Christian believer's hope.

There is no room for smug complacency here. It is not that you have picked a winner, but that a winner has picked you. All that you can do is be grateful and remain faithful. And remaining faithful will require you to act according to the law of love.

Let me close this circle – which opened with an excerpt from Rabbi Kushner's book – by recalling the words of the prophet Micah, words that are applicable today, of course, to both Christians and Jews:

You have been told, O man, what is good,
    and what the Lord requires of you:
Only to do right and to love goodness,
    and to walk humbly with your God. (6:8)

That sounds to me like the basis of a spirituality capable of transforming both persons and workplaces in a world where bad things can happen to anyone, but where everyone can survive and even prosper by simply choosing to 'walk humbly' with God.

PART TWO

DEALING WITH WORKPLACE WOUNDS

CHAPTER FOUR
CRITICISM

Is there anyone alive who has never been criticised unfairly, misunderstood, passed over, forgotten, betrayed? Probably not. Certainly, an incalculable number of these 'criticism' wounds are inflicted in the workplace every day.

Such criticism can be harsh. It is, all too often, compounded by false accusations and subtle forms of sabotage. Feelings of fear, anger, and shame often accompany workplace criticism, singly or in combination, and these emotions will always be there. How, then, should you prepare to deal with any of these workplace wounds?

Spirituality can help you handle problems arising from criticism on the job; it gives you strength and enables you to keep these setbacks in perspective. Spirituality provides answers from within – that is, from within your own soul.

COMING TO (PSYCHOLOGICAL) BLOWS

Conflict is a 'given' in the workplace, we are told. That may be so, but the nature of the conflict, and the way we respond to it, often speaks volumes about our relationships with those around us. A young woman who had worked as an administrative assistant once told me that an exchange with a rude, overbearing female bank branch manager nearly led to the inflicting of physical wounds.

The assistant was working with adding-machine tapes and happened to have a scissors in her hand when she was berated unfairly for a mistake in computing the total of a column of numbers. As it happened, this young woman had not been re-sponsible for the error in question. All the same, a high decibel volley of verbal abuse issued forth from the manager's desk. This prompted the assistant to stand, tapes and scissors in hand, to attempt a clarification. The manager recoiled in hor-ror, thinking she was about to be stabbed!

'I could never have done that,' the assistant told me, 'although I wanted to!' Instead, she dropped everything, including the scissors, and quit on the spot. Perhaps the reaction was extreme, perhaps it wasn't. Make no mistake, such tense situations in the workplace represent forms of spiritual and psychological violence, even if no physical blows occur.

After some reflection and soul searching, the young woman decided to use the concept of 'human dignity' as her range finder in the search for new employment. Now she works as an office manager in a family-owned construction company, a place where, in her words, 'they treat you like a human being'. There are career counsellors who will tell you that the failure to develop 'conflict management skills' is a significant hazard to career growth. This may well be so, but ignoring the 'treat-me-like-a-human-being' standard in one's workplace life may be an even more imposing career hazard.

BEYOND THE STIFF UPPER LIP

'It's all part of the job. Either you can take it or you can't.' This commonly expressed sentiment is not, perhaps, the most effective in formulating a long-term strategy for dealing with invasive, painful workplace criticism.

It is worth remembering that there are occasional violent deaths in the workplace. They are rare enough to be considered newsworthy, and thus, paradoxically, become major influences on the way some of us view the workplace. ('If it bleeds, it leads', is the principle of selection guiding the decisions of many local television and tabloid news editors, a philosophy consistent with the values of the Interest-Excitement culture that drive that industry.) More often than not, though, workplace violence is related to off-the-job problems.

The wounds under consideration in this and the following short chapters happen on the job; they are occasioned by emotions and events in the workplace. They are not physical; neither are the bandages that spirituality can provide to help you tend to them. They are nevertheless quite real, and ignoring them – or attempting to pretend that they don't exist – can be a huge mistake.

In considering emotional wounds in general, I think of a connection Shakespeare makes in *Othello*, Act II, Scene iii, where he has Iago say to Roderigo, 'How poor are they that have not patience! What wound did ever heal but by degrees?' Iago's sinister role in the play should not blind us to the wisdom of these words. Here as elsewhere in the play, the bard makes the creative choice of using perhaps his greatest villain to pass along eminently sound counsel.

Any wound, physical or psychological, needs time to heal. (Later in this same speech, Iago refers to it pointedly as 'dilatory Time'.) If an injury is to heal, it must indeed heal 'by degrees'. And it takes patience, one of the Pauline Criteria, to permit this to happen.

Patience, you will recall, implies a certain amount of suffering. No one instinctively *welcomes* suffering (even in the relatively mild form of patience), but suffering is easier to bear if it is accepted as necessary to heal a particular wound. And patience, you must never forget, implies full acceptance of a problem, not an attempt to rationalise away its existence.

RESPONDING TO CRITICISM

In one of Lord George Gordon Byron's poems, there is a memorable description of an eagle being wounded by a 'fatal dart', a dart guided in its lethal trajectory by one of that eagle's own feathers. It is important to bear in mind, in dealing with the problems of workplace criticism, that you can bring – or help to bring – the wound on yourself. Clearly, this is a point to be pondered as you consider the 'darts' others may send your way during the working day. Listen to Lord Byron:

'Twas thine own genius gave the final blow,
And help'd to plant the wound that laid thee low:
So the struck eagle, stretched upon the plain,
No more through rolling clouds to soar again,
View'd his own feather on the fatal dart,
And wing'd the shaft that quiver'd in his heart;

Keen were his pangs, but keener far to feel
He nursed the pinion which impell'd the steel;
While the same plumage that had warm'd his nest
Drank the last life-drop of his bleeding breast.
— ('English Bards and Scotch Reviewers', lines 819–28)

The recognition of your own 'genius' as something capable of enhancing a wound is a very healthy, if humbling, gift.

As the recognition that you are responsible for how you react to the 'darts' of others dawns on you, it can indeed give rise to some keen pangs. Usually, the wounds you associate with criticism are not exactly fatal; you can surely 'soar again', if not through 'rolling clouds', at least along the high road of reconnection and recovery. But it will all take time.

Perhaps some of your own habitual ways of evaluating workplace situations enhances or strengthens cycles of criticism you experience from others in the workplace. If you've become accustomed to saying, 'Time is money', why not try a variation on that theme? Try this experiment. Say, if only to yourself, 'Time is patience, and it takes both time and patience for any wound to heal'.

THE POWER OF PRAISE

'Spray the place with praise', a wise elder executive once advised a young manager. The older man was not suggesting flattery; just honest recognition, positive reinforcement, respectful affirmation and constructive appraisal.

Criticism usually takes the opposite route. Public criticism makes the negativity visible and audible, all to the embarrassment of the person being criticised. Unfair criticism (rarely regarded as such by the busy or preoccupied person issuing it) compounds the humiliation by adding the dimension of injustice.

Even someone who is 'addicted' to criticism can be transformed by a few moments of heartfelt, reality-based public praise from a colleague. (If you never receive it, you can hardly know how to give it!) This is a strategy fully in keeping with the Pauline notion of love, and worth considering closely as you reflect on your day-to-day dealing with hypercritical colleagues.

FORMAL EVALUATION, INFORMAL EVALUATION

It is routine in the workplace to assess performance against pre-established norms and mutually understood expectations. This can be an ideal forum for constructive criticism. Most supervisors tend to put assessment off, however, simply because they are uneasy doing it. Excessive *supervision* is often found in organisations suffering from an absence of corporate *vision*. So a tendency to postpone formal assessment of the persons a manager is responsible for supervising is not necessarily a bad thing. It could be associated with managers caught up in forward, visionary thinking. He or she communicates both vision and enthusiasm and prefers to cheer employees on as a team, rather than measuring individual performance step by step by means of a formal performance-review mechanism. This kind of manager exhibits trust, which, in turn, almost always stimulates productivity.

Such a manager, however, like the parent of an adolescent, has to face the problem of figuring out where trust ends and neglect begins. This is never an easy task, and may best be regarded as an ongoing series of adjustments, rather than a single 'policy' that can be 'implemented' and then forgotten.

Some species of 'formal' constructive criticism will always be part of workplace life. If this criticism

- ¬ is balanced;
- ¬ takes place within a supportive informal day-to-day workplace environment;
- ¬ takes the form of a formal, scheduled, straightforward exchange, and;
- ¬ is handled professionally and with a measure of encouragement by the person passing along the information, then it is unlikely that any but the thinnest of skins will be wounded in the process.

It is important, however, that both the giver and receiver of formal constructive criticism make an effort to remain calm and clear during these exchanges. A minimal amount of 'strategic preparation' for the meeting will usually do the trick here.

Don't assume the worst before any meeting meant to help you focus on performance issues; if you do, you may *bring about* the worst. Just as you cannot see the bottom of a pool or lake when the waters are agitated, you will never see assessment issues without distortion if either party to the evaluation conversation is emotionally upset. By the same token, if nothing at all by way of measurement norms is set out clearly beforehand, on paper, for both to see, then agitation or emotional turmoil is much more likely to result.

SERENITY: THE BEST RESPONSE TO WORDS MEANT TO HURT

Workplace wounds induced by conscious, hurtful criticism can be incubated in jealousy and spite, transmitted by direct verbal attack, or passed along indirectly through anonymous (almost always cowardly) notes or cutting remarks overheard or reported at second or third hand. If you encounter such criticism, how will you react?

Fighting vitriol with vitriol is not a good idea. Serenity (not to be confused with stony silence) is an excellent defence, one that is firmly rooted in the Pauline value of self-control. *Don't pursue conflict for its own sake.* If others are present, a simple question directed to them, for example, 'Do you agree with that?' can help put everything in the proper context.

If you are faced with unfair, even abusive criticism from a colleague who approaches you one-on-one, your strategy is simple: listen. Be sure you hear what is being said. Repeat it aloud.

If what is being said is untrue and a threat to your career, reduce what you heard to writing, add your explanatory or defensive commentary, and ask to have a conversation with your immediate supervisor. And by the way, cultivate the habit of 'listening generously', a quality that career expert Lynne

Waymon recommends, in good times and in bad, for all who interact in the workplace.

In the matter of unfair criticism, as in so many other unpleasant workplace situations (particularly when you are caught in an ethical dilemma), your best response – one that will be made easier by your reliance on and cultivation of self-control – is to avoid responding in kind to your accuser. Beyond that, if you face a truly serious situation, you should consider taking the one-level-up route: talk to your immediate boss. If your immediate boss is the problem, go up another level or more until you connect with a responsible person who can hear you out. If you are the CEO and the problem is your chairman, take it to your board!

If what is being said is untrue but not a threat to your employment, or not worth alerting higher-ups about, reject the criticism firmly. Do this without emotion and without discussion. If someone rolls a ball in your direction, you will not have a game of catch unless you pick up the ball. Once again, self-control will be an essential part of your response.

It will usually be easy to reject the criticism but difficult not to reject the person. Try always to keep the door between you open. Face up to the difficulty as best you can, and always leave yourself open to an apology. Always.

If what is being said is true, even though the message was rudely served up by a person who has no right to criticise you, talk it over with a trusted friend in or out of the workplace. Hard as it is to take at times, the truth can always help you.

If the message was anonymous or communicated to you by a third party who received it in confidence, give it the same validity test sketched out above and act accordingly. Either take it to heart or toss it in the wastebasket. Then move on. And by the way, if you have high visibility as a manager, there are ways of getting the word out that you never read anonymous mail. Provide an ombudsman if your organisation is large and complex; anonymity should always be offered to conscientious whistle-blowers. But if it is known throughout your organisation that anonymous communications will be filtered and normally not get through to you, crank complaints will diminish, as will interference with your sleep. And take this tip: a good sleep-preserving principle for the busy manager is never to read any mail after 5:00 p.m.

Surely, there is nothing wrong with you if you are sensitive, even thin-skinned. Thin-skinned people can benefit from the reminder that spirituality emanates from within, from within the soul. And if the skin, as the saying goes, 'is the surface of the mind, and the mind is the surface of the soul', thin-skinned people have an advantage — faster access to the soul, which is the ultimate repository for answers from within.

INNERCISE

Just as physical exercise tones up both the muscles and the skin, spiritual exercise (some call it 'innercise') can strengthen the soul against any possible workplace wound, including, of course, the wound of criticism.

Fitness-conscious persons are conscientious about working out, often every day. Anyone concerned about spiritual fitness should be just as conscientious about 'working in'. This commitment means a regimen of some form of daily prayer. Your commitment should also include reflective reading, and ongoing reminders to yourself about the importance of listening to God's voice in the circumstances of your life, and seeing God's hand in the wonders of creation.

If the physically fit, because of repeated physical exercise, enjoy a longer life expectancy, it seems logical to suggest a spiritual parallel. The inner spiritual life may have been on Robert Frost's mind when he saw the possibility of an 'answer from within'. If, in the face of criticism, you find that you have nothing to draw upon from within, the situation you face is clear. You have some innercising to do.

In anticipating future criticism, give some thought to these words from the famous peace prayer of St Francis of Assisi: 'Grant that I may not so much seek to be understood as to understand'. And from that same prayer: 'Where there is hatred, let me sow love'. Let these petitions sink into your soul so that they can become principles to guide your response to workplace criticism.

CHAPTER FIVE
FEAR

Fear is usually a self-inflicted wound. It is intimately related to worry, and worry almost always arises over something that does not exist (or, at the very least, no *longer* exists, or does not yet – and may never – exist). Many wise people have weighed in over the years with the observation that fear is the opposite of love, the first Pauline principle. Not all our workplace exchanges, of course, are driven by love. But it's hard to imagine a workplace relationship that would not benefit from a commitment to renew the value of non-exploitative, accepting love, the kind of love that reflects God's love for us.

FEAR REFLECTED ON ITSELF

A perceptive man who runs a high technology firm was described to me as one who knows humans as well as he knows the newest of the new technology. He understands the people who create, use, and are affected by that technology. On one occasion, he wondered whether an employee, who was experiencing serious performance problems and whom he was eager to help, was suffering from some kind of attention-deficit disorder.

Psychological tests revealed no problem. The employee tested well cognitively and gave no evidence of being out of touch with reality. He lacked confidence, however, and was distressed because he always seemed to be convinced that something was wrong with him. This employee was worrying about his worrying.

Only after medical and psychiatric evaluations validated his health could the employee be persuaded to use the knowledge that he was healthy to free himself from worry. Before this reassurance, he was both healthy (although unconvinced that he was) and distressed (because he thought he had something to worry about). Once convinced that he had no health problems, he could accept a physician's instruction and the unremitting encouragement of his boss to stop worrying and take control. It took him a while to learn that worry typically looks to a past that is dead, or a future that may not happen as the worrier envisions it. Worry has an insidious capacity to pull the worrier out of the present, the only place where he or she does, in fact, exist.

Recall that President Franklin Delano Roosevelt, in his inaugural address on 4 March 1933, chose to 'assert my firm belief' that 'the only thing we have to fear is fear itself'. And Roosevelt immediately added that fear is a 'nameless, unreasoning, unjustified terror which paralyses needed efforts to convert retreat into advance'.

Having nothing to fear but fear itself may have been what Ralph Waldo Emerson was suggesting in a little poem titled 'Borrowing', which is included in his 'Quatrains':

> Some of your hurts you have cured,
>   And the sharpest you still have survived,
> But what torments of grief you endured
>   From evils which never arrived!

You can save yourself a good deal of the 'grief' Emerson mentions by simply maintaining a sensible, prudent and balanced present orientation. Embracing the present moment with love (the first Pauline value), patience (the fourth), and faithfulness (the seventh) will go a long way towards helping you to banish fear and worry from your workplace life.

FEAR TAKES MANY FORMS

Workplace fear can take the form of a fear of discovery, fear of failure, fear of criticism, fear of loss of job, or fear of what others might think.

If your fear of discovery relates to criminal behaviour, get a lawyer. If it is fear of something actually or possibly unethical coming to light, talk first to an adviser whom you trust and next to a responsible person within the organisation.

Understand, however, that most of us spend too much time worrying about the discovery of minor lapses and honest errors in judgement – problems that take more effort and energy to conceal than they are worth. If the actions that concern you fall into this category, remind yourself that nobody is perfect and then address this question to yourself: 'What is the worst that could happen if I shared this problem openly with all the affected parties?'

If it is failure that you fear, recognise that not everything depends on you. You have associates (the preferred term now for 'employees' in a growing number of organisations) ready to work along with you if you let them know you are open to collaboration. A workplace touched by the spirituality discussed in Chapter One will be an increasingly collaborative rather than a destructively competitive place. Your own experience and commitment to spiritual values can free you up to begin the 'ally relationship' your current project may demand. And remember: the spirituality I've invited you to consider will sustain you in the midst of uncertainty; it will shore up your faith in yourself as well as in God.

Unbelievers never try, but even believers of long standing have difficulty in accepting as personally applicable to themselves the word of God in scriptural expressions like these:

I have the strength for everything through him who empowers me. (Philippians 4:11-13)

Entrust your works to the Lord
and your plans will succeed. (Proverbs 16:3)

Any believer can bring these words to bear in daily life by grounding them on the absolute, faith-based conviction that God is with and within him or her all the time.

God is interested in and engaged with you in whatever is happening to or through you at any particular moment. The spirituality you bring with you into the workplace can be expected to heighten your awareness of an active God at work in the world, who wants to work through you. You have nothing to fear. Recall that fear itself is all you have to fear, and then say, with the psalmist:

> Prosper the work of our hands! Prosper the work of our hands! (Psalm 90:17)

If you take this approach, criticism and censure, and even the possibility of career disruptions, will seem less threatening than they would to a person with lots of fears and little faith. Know that God is with you at all times, and that your conscious concern to reflect God's love in the world will help you clear the hurdles and overcome the obstacles that will always be a part of working life.

A LESSON

Take a lesson from the life of my friend Lillian Brill. This lesson came to me directly from her, by word and example, shortly before she died. It embodies a spiritual principle that served her well both in life and death, but especially in life, in the many workplaces that were enriched by her competent and caring presence as an army nurse.

Lillian had an abiding conviction that God could never let her down, could never be anything but faithful to his promise to love her and be with her, no matter what.

She was ill, more so than I realised, when she gave me a cheerful telephone call one morning to say she wanted me to officiate at her funeral. 'Nothing sad or solemn,' she said, 'I want it to be a happy celebration.' She asked that I drive over from Washington, DC, to see her at her home in Annapolis, Maryland, a day or two after her next monthly blood transfusion ('my cocktail party'), which was part of her battle against Hodgkin's disease.

Lillian wanted me to help her plan the funeral liturgy. She asked that I bring another friend, Elaine Walter, dean of the School of Music at The Catholic University of America where Lillian had studied nursing.

'I love the violin', Lillian reminded Elaine as our planning session began in her brightly decorated waterside cottage. It was a very pleasant, sunny, morning in the middle of the week. Elaine assured her that the violin would have a prominent place in the programme of music; Lillian specified selections she would like included in the programme.

Turning to me, this retired US Army colonel, who looked vibrant and not at all close to death, asked if the Mass could be celebrated in the nearby US Naval Academy Chapel where, in retirement, she often worshiped. I assured her that this could be easily arranged. Then she said, 'As I told you on the phone, no gloom, no doom. Keep it light and make it a genuine celebration. You see, for years I've been paging through the Bible and pausing to underline those sections where God makes promises to his people. You'd have trouble counting all those promises of fidelity and salvation.'

Then she came to her central point: 'And if God is God, he can't be anything but faithful to his promises. So what do I have to fear?'

She died three weeks later. Her funeral went exactly as planned. I had the honour of letting Lillian deliver the homily at her own funeral. All I did was spell out for those who gathered in remembrance and celebration of her life, the invaluable lesson Lillian taught me when she uttered those two memorable sentences about God's promises to his people.

OVERCOMING FEAR

Each time you overcome fear of any kind – picking up that heavyweight telephone on your desk to make a call you are afraid of placing; seeing your doctor when you fear the news will not be good; asking for the sale when you are worried about a turndown; exposing yourself to the possibility of criticism or rejection; facing up to whatever it is that tends to immobilise you – each time you overcome fears like these you are a freer, fuller person.

On a completely worldly, totally secular level, you are a better, more productive person, more fully engaged with practical reality. On the spiritual level, facing up to fear is your way of affirming your belief that God is there at your side, standing by you in the troubling circumstance, with you all the way.

The collected spiritual wisdom of the ages puts this simple question to you every moment of your waking life: if God is with you, who can be against you?

Take a moment now to attend to that question. I believe that once you do, you will be inspired to live the rest of your life with the obvious and only possible answer to that question echoing in your heart. Let your response activate the love, patience and faithfulness that will, along with the other Pauline principles, become for you a matter of habit rooted deep within your soul.

ATTITUDE

Dealing with fear through the values of love, faithfulness and quiet courage, as Lillian Brill did, is all a question of attitude. And you are in charge of your attitudes.

The word itself suggests a tilt, a slant, a leaning towards. You can choose to be positive or negative, upbeat or downcast, hopeful or pessimistic, fearful or peaceful. No one but you can determine how you will 'trim your sails' to navigate the troubled waters that can swirl around you at any time.

The following anonymous reflection was under the desktop glass close to the telephone Kevin Dolan used during his transition period from a good job just lost, to another not yet found. It helped to overcome the fear he felt that he would never find another good job:

> The longer I live, the more I realise the impact of attitude on life. Attitude is more important than facts. It is more important than the past, than education, than money, than circumstances, than failures, than successes, than what other people think of, say, or do. It is more important than appearance, giftedness, or skill. It will make or break a company, a school, or a home. The remarkable thing is we have a choice every day regarding the attitude we will embrace. We cannot change our past ... We cannot change

the fact that people will act in a certain way. We cannot change the inevitable. The only thing we can do is to play on the string we have. And that is our attitude. I am convinced that life is 10 per cent what happens to me and 90 per cent how I react to it. And so it is with you ... We are in charge of our attitudes.

There is no question about it. You are in charge of your attitudes. And you are doing yourself no favour by permitting an attitude of fearfulness to paralyse you.

Repeat the questioning process outlined in this chapter as many times as necessary, and don't be surprised to learn that 'necessary' means at regular or irregular intervals for the rest of your life. If God is really with you (your faith assures you this is so), who can be against you? The answer to that question has to come from within. Search your soul for the answer. If you find yourself coming up empty, keep searching. You may discover the need to do some prayerful listening to scripture: to the psalms, to the Sermon on the Mount, or to other sources of reassurance available to you in the inspired word of God. Use them to fill up that seemingly empty centre of your soul. It will not stay empty for long.

I have often remarked to myself how perceptive is playwright Robert Bolt's observation: 'It is with us as it is with our cities: an accelerating flight to the periphery, leaving a centre that is empty when the hours of business are over.' Fear is often indicative of an empty centre, a vacuum in the soul. Surely, God intends no one to live this way. God does intend, however, that you listen to his word, internalise it, and let it drive fears from your soul, shape your attitudes, and guide your choices.

I can think of no better way to close this discussion of fear than to repeat the advice from Proverbs, and urge you, too, to repeat it often: 'Entrust your works to the Lord, and your plans will succeed' (Proverbs 16:3).

CHAPTER SIX
BETRAYAL

This workplace wound presents itself, more readily than most, for interpretation and treatment within the framework of Christian spirituality. When the average person, religious or not, hears the word 'betrayal', there is a tendency to associate it more or less automatically with the name 'Judas'.

Anyone even vaguely familiar with the story of the life of Jesus knows that Judas betrayed him. It is also understood that some equivalent of the gospel's 'thirty pieces of silver' – in other words, some form of greed, gain, or self-promotion – can usually explain the betrayer's motivation. Weakness of character, comparable to that shown by Judas Iscariot, may also contribute to the betrayer's unprincipled act.

Whatever the explanation, betrayal happens in the workplace and its victims suffer. Put yourself in the shoes of anyone who has experienced betrayal; you may not have to go far beyond your own clothes closet to find a good fit!

If you need an example, however, I can offer one. Consider the case of a manager I know, a seasoned professional who was encouraged to be candid and completely frank with the selection committee reviewing inside candidates for promotion to an executive-level position reporting directly to the CEO. As requested, she was disarmingly direct in assessing her strengths and weaknesses, as well as the strengths and weaknesses in the substance and style of the CEO's approach to management. She did this to lay out a framework within which their relative strengths and weaknesses could be matched up, and some judgements made concerning the likelihood of a good 'fit', a positive working relationship, if she were selected for the position.

Someone on the selection committee broke the presumably unshakable commitment of confidentiality that had been touted during her interview as an integral part of the selection process. That unknown someone disclosed to the CEO all the 'negatives' in the candidate's assessment of his management record. Instead of a promotion, the candidate got a summons to appear before the CEO, explain her disloyalty and defend her right to continued employment in her present job.

Needless to say, she felt betrayed. She remains in the job, considering herself now to be 'unpromotable' in that organisation and doomed to a distant but 'correct' relationship with the boss as long as she remains there. She may well leave the firm someday. When and if she does, she probably will not get a glowing reference from the CEO. Perhaps more important, she will now no longer be trusting and instead 'careful' all the time. Sad.

For another example of workplace betrayal, consider the case of the designer of a major corporation's information management system. He was given confidential orders, in light of a board-level downsizing decision, to reconfigure the system and write out (that is, eliminate) many jobs. He carried out this sensitive assignment well and without breaching the trust that had been accorded him. He was well aware that his own job *title* would be eliminated in the restructuring, but it never occurred to him that he himself would wind up on the street. He simply assumed, in view of the fact that the application of his talent to this assignment would save the corporation $6 million, that there would be a place for him on the scaled-down organisation's management team. Not so. They let him go. He went away mad; he felt betrayed.

TRUST LOST
Trust is almost always a casualty in any betrayal situation. Betrayal of trust means broken promises, trashed agreements, reversal of assurances. It means abdication of the basic responsibilities of friendship: dependability and reliability. At bottom, betrayal is a refusal to love, but that dimension of the reality is hardly ever recognised when it happens.

Curiously, the victim of betrayal will often feel shame, a shame that is not totally dissimilar to that which is sometimes felt by those who experience rape. Some people react to job loss that is totally without fault on their part with a feeling of profound shame.

Shame is a very tricky affect; it lowers the eyes, drops the head, and promotes withdrawal. Shame tends to immobilise a person; it can be profoundly debilitating.

Shame is not the only possible reaction to betrayal, of course. Workplace betrayers may send their victims into sudden torrents of fury. The anger that is triggered by betrayal often precipitates an immediate but unwise response to the situation.

When betrayed, you must not yield to either shame or rage. You have to find a way to let the Pauline value of self-control guide you back towards a necessary balance.

If you permit the emotional volcano that follows betrayal to turn in on itself, you run the risk of depression. If you release that energy in the form of anger and strike back at the betrayer or simply vent your rage, you lose control (and thus diminish your humanity). You also further pollute the very workplace environment that your vocation is calling you to make more civil, and cordial, and human.

What, then, are you to do when you are betrayed?

THE EXAMPLE OF JESUS

Jesus knew who his betrayer was. He permitted Judas to greet and kiss him. Listen to what Jesus said to the man who 'sold him out': 'Friend, do what you have come for' (Matthew 26:50). There is sadness and resignation in that line, but no hint of anger or revenge. Sure, it saddened him to know that a member of his trusted inner circle was about to betray him. And there you have a clue: a managed sadness, far stronger than anger, is the appropriate response to betrayal.

Jesus moved on with what he had to do, but he remained wide open and completely ready to forgive. Asking for or receiving forgiveness was not his problem; that was up to Judas. Being prepared to forgive, and being ready to deal constructively with the effects of betrayal, is the challenge that can only be met by the one who was or is about to be betrayed.

Just a few lines after this account of the exchange between Jesus and Judas in Matthew's Gospel, you will find the famous saying of Jesus: 'Put your sword back into its sheath, for all who take the sword will perish by the sword' (26:52). If you have experienced betrayal first hand, this gospel message is worth considering closely. If you try to live by the 'sword' of retaliation in the workplace, you will surely 'die' a workplace death by someone else's sword. Recall the Pauline Criteria: love, joy, peace, patience, kindness, generosity, faithfulness, gentleness, self-control. These values (in this case, especially self-control) are your arms and armour. Your use of them will not only preserve your workplace life, but encourage others there to equip themselves in similar fashion.

WHAT TO DO
As in the case of unfair criticism, the one-level-up approach should be taken as you move on with life, choosing the higher road as your route to recovery from the damaging effects of betrayal. Consider the following true story, however, where the problem existed one level up with a hostile board of directors, and there was no higher level where the score could be settled. There was no principled, neutral superior to whom to appeal. So the betrayed person just decided to move on.

He was a chairman and chief executive officer who had hit all performance targets, met the goals set for him by the board, and delivered impressive results to the bottom line. When he asked the board for reciprocity and complained about the hostility they were showing him, the ranking member snapped, 'What did you expect me and the rest of us to be, a friend? If you want a friend, get a dog'. Thus, the CEO's many contributions were reduced to a single, sadistic and not all that original joke. Ever since millions of moviegoers first heard it in the film *Wall Street*, the 'get a dog' rejoinder is commonly used to justify inhumane and abusive treatment in the workplace.

Some workplace environments are poisoned, not worth saving. You simply have to move on. Once you move on, you can further free yourself by exercising the self-control that enables you to stop talking about it. Let it ride. Get on with your life.

A really well-functioning spirituality will have freed you up enough to forgive. Remember that the virtue of self-control is the one you rely on most heavily in betrayal situations. Use it to overcome the temptation to attack the motives and character of your betrayers. You should even be able to boast (to yourself, at least) about your willingness to forgive. Your refusal to speak ill of those who turned against you will bear quiet, eloquent witness to the forgiveness you have given. And there lies a measure of both your largeness of heart and the depth of your humanity. Every betrayal carries with it an opportunity for growth.

'AND ON THE NIGHT HE WAS BETRAYED, HE TOOK BREAD ...'

If you need a story to help you wrap your mind around the issue of betrayal and how to grow through it, recall the gospel story of the betrayal of Jesus. What can you learn from this unparalleled example?

Christians, in their eucharistic celebrations, remember Jesus 'in the breaking of the bread'. They give thanks for the good that came to them out of his betrayal. They focus on the verbs in the scriptural accounts, a focus that can be helpful to anyone trying to deal with betrayal. The gospel accounts say he 'took', 'blessed', 'broke', and 'gave' bread to his closest friends – his associates, his com-panions – after first 'giving thanks' to the Creator of everything: bread, friendship, and, indeed, life itself.

You, too, in your own time, have to give thanks, even in the wake of betrayal. Take ahold of the 'bread' of daily existence, even when it includes the experience of betrayal, and bless it. A blessing means saying something good about that which is blessed. (Literally, a blessing is a *bene-dictio*, a 'well-saying'.) Whatever you face, it somehow comes from God who at least permits it and thus can draw good from it. Then break the loaf of reality that is yours, break it open so that you can in some way give it (and yourself) to your brothers and sisters in the human community. You will encounter your segment of that community in workplace, or family, or wherever you happen to be. And that is precisely where you have to share – to give fully and generously of yourself.

BEYOND THE PAIN

Betrayal, badly managed, can become an enemy within. That is the only way it will ever really hurt you. 'We are betrayed', wrote the poet George Meredith, 'by what is false within'. You can be hurt only if you let that falsehood – the injustice, the hatred – reside within. Remember, betrayal is at bottom a refusal to love. If you find yourself, when betrayed, refusing to love, you are not only ignoring the first of the Pauline principles, you are falling into a trap set for you by the enemy. Your spirituality is there to remind you that you can do far, far better than that!

> Straight are the paths of the Lord, in them the just walk, but sinners stumble in them. (Hosea 14:10)

CHAPTER SEVEN
FALSE ACCUSATIONS

A false accusation is always unjust. It differs from criticism because there is no element – or even possibility – of truth in a false accusation. Such accusations are a form of betrayal, but they are not necessarily related to the prior condition of trust or friendship that makes betrayal so hard to take. A false accusation is simply a lie. And it wounds.

IMMEDIATE RESPONSES

It was not a false accusation, just an unspoken question, when a high school teacher, a friend of mine, turned quickly and caught the eye of a student who could possibly have tossed a wet wad of paper that had just hit the blackboard.

'It wasn't me, sir', the student blurted out.

'It wasn't *I*', said the teacher in his unflagging commitment to correct grammar.

'I know it wasn't you, sir, but it wasn't me neither', said the anxious youngster – for whom, at that moment, the establishment of innocence was clearly more important than correct English.

There will be moments in your life when, with or without fault on the part of another, you will be falsely accused; not just questioned or suspected, but charged falsely. You may be totally convinced, absolutely sure, that 'it wasn't I'. But someone will assert the contrary. Although your instinct will be to brand your accuser as a liar, that person may not necessarily be lying. To say something that turns out to be incorrect is not necessarily to have lied. A lie is a statement (or an expression like a nod of the head) that conveys to someone who has a right to know the opposite of what, in your mind, you know to be true. When you say you spoke to someone last Tuesday, and the conversation actually took place on Wednesday, you are not lying; you are just confused. If you stole a sum of money and, upon inquiry by authorities deny it, you are both a thief and a liar.

There is a genteel kind of false accusation that floats like a feather in virtually every workplace. More gossipy than accusatory, attributions of motivation, for instance, are blithely made without any knowledge at all of what actually is happening in the mind and heart of the person who is presumed, for some unflattering reason, to be doing this or that. Public figures live with this and have no recourse to legal protection from libel. Private persons intent on minding their own business are often wounded by others who prefer not to mind theirs, and act, for all the world, as though they were omniscient.

They think they can read the minds and motives of others and disclose whatever they think they have 'read' in others. This curious reading habit is not prompted by a love of learning. It can be explained only in terms of pettiness, insecurity, envy, curiosity, boredom, jealousy, hatred, or some combination of these elements, and more.

More destructive forms of false accusation, in the style made famous by 'honest' Iago, happen all the time. These accusations not only wound, they kill. Othello, you will recall, believed his trusted friend, the mendacious Iago, so Desdemona died. There may or may not be workplace fatalities associated with false accusations, but the 'death' of your ability to trust and deal openly with others is certainly at issue in such situations. Your good name, too, of course, is under attack.

Your proper and immediate concern, upon learning that you have been falsely accused, is with reputation only if you are lucky; it could be your career that is now in danger. You have to act to defend yourself whenever reputation, career, or more is at stake.

JUST THE FACTS
There is nothing like a fact to dispose of a falsehood. If you are accused of having said or done something you did not do, post

proof that will defend you. It is not always possible to prove what you did not say or do; it is easier to find documentation for and witness to what you in fact did do or say.

These, of course, are steps you must take when you are under direct assault. Your aim is to defend yourself, not to retaliate or to prove to the whole world that you know 'why' your accuser acts as he or she does. Avoid mud-wrestling in the motivation pit.

Just as others cannot with certainty read your mind, you cannot know for sure why they are doing this to you. Better to let your character stand up in your defence. At the end of the day, your own integrity will prove to be your best shield.

The way you conduct yourself in the workplace is, in fact, your character in motion. People will have noticed this, simply because it is impossible for you to go unnoticed wherever you work. You may be unappreciated, but not unnoticed. Others have been observing you every day, just as you have been observing them. They make judgements about you, just as you make judgements about them. And those judgements can be wrong, either way. Moreover, these judgements are so much a part of human nature and so often neutral in their evaluative dimensions that you don't give them a second thought. They do, however, contribute towards the gradual formation of your impression of another person, distinctive if not detailed. The way you carry yourself – indeed, the emotional reaction you bring to the accusations you face – will say a great deal about you to others who will be drawing their own conclusions from your accuser's charges.

Just as you should gather proof in your own defence, a false accuser should be challenged to post proof in support of the false charges. But in the absence of proof, the jury of your workplace peers will always find in your favour because of the person they know you to be.

When the Pauline values become part of you, you are, unlike Iago, an honest person, a person of integrity. You do not merely *seem* trustworthy, as Iago did. (About Iago, the tragically misled Othello said: 'This honest creature doubtless/Sees and knows more, much more than he unfolds.') You are in *fact* honest – a person of integrity. Your reputation and your career will withstand the assault of any false accusation – not because of what you say, but because of who you are.

Someone who is not guided by love, joy, peace, patience, kindness, generosity, faithfulness, gentleness and self-control is, of course, a person for whom issues of character and integrity are of secondary (or even lower) importance. Someone who is not an honest person will probably overreact to accusations; such a person will 'protest too much', and quite likely lose some ground with respect to both reputation and career, regardless of the truth or falsehood in the accusation.

Keep in mind Horace Greeley's wise observation: 'Fame is a vapour, popularity an accident, riches take wings. Only one thing endures, and that is character.'

Most people are good people, but most people also believe what they want to believe. They will want to believe you, if they see you as a person of integrity. They will grow skeptical indeed if you give them reason to believe that you are a hypocrite, presenting only the image of a positive character while dishonestly defending yourself against what might be a true accusation. The truth or falsehood of the charge pales in significance when compared to the truth or falsehood of who you are.

SPIRITUAL FOUNDATIONS
The unfortunate fact remains that some bad people – not just selfish and mean-spirited people, but bad people, evil people – are out there. They are capable, for motives you may never discover, of knowingly speaking falsely about you. Practically, how are you going to handle that? You can only speculate about that now. But you can also plan to build a spiritual infrastructure that will include peace, patience and self-control, upon which any practical plan of action or inaction can rest.

I sat in a courtroom for one full day some years ago to observe part of what proved to be a six-week trial. The defendant, a personal friend, was then a public official, who was falsely accused by persons of questionable credibility, and later acquitted of bribery and extortion charges.

The prosecution put his ex-wife on the stand and subjected her to extensive questioning about family and financial matters. Her former husband, the defendant, was visibly angry at the government lawyers for putting her through this ordeal. If looks could kill, there would have been murder charges leveled against him as he stared at the prosecuting attorney when all of us rose for a recess as the witness was excused.

My friend had long been angry over the false accusations that led up to this trial. He was now outraged over the grilling to which his former wife had been subjected. During the break, he and I spoke briefly. I said, 'Come up with an image of tranquility. Fix it in your mind and have it there when the trial resumes and you sit down again at the defence table. Don't let them see how upset you are; control the impulse to fight back. Think of a calm lake, a snow-capped mountain, a bed of yellow roses, a sunset, a field of wheat. Think of anything that will calm you down and enable you to sit there in some semblance of peace and dignity.'

I didn't want him to risk upsetting anyone else, particularly the judge and jury. Two weeks later, after the acquittal, several jurors told reporters that they thought this witness had been treated badly and that her divorce from the defendant had nothing to do with the issues to be decided in the trial. Moreover, one juror added that when the defendant eventually took the stand in his own defence, he, as she perceived him, was 'incapable of lying; mistakes in judgement, maybe, but no lies'.

If, in response to false accusations and treatment that you know is unfair, you lose control, you may be giving away your best chance for eventual vindication. This is not to say never protest; it is only to say never choose, under emotional pressure, to lose your balance. Choose instead to fix your attention on an image of tranquility. And give some thought to an act of forgiveness.

The vengeful will suffer the Lord's vengeance, for he remembers their sins in detail. Forgive your neighbour's injustice; then when you pray, your own sins will be forgiven. (Sirach 28:1-2)

CHAPTER EIGHT
INGRATITUDE

When those who supervise your work or receive the services you render never express appreciation, you notice it. You resent the ingratitude. It can hurt. Your reaction can range from annoyance to anger, from silence to sarcasm. No one likes to be taken for granted.

What's more, no one, deep down, wants to be regarded as 'only being in it for the money'. The money is not unimportant, of course, but the purpose of work is a great deal broader than simple financial remuneration.

This 'something broader' relates to meeting a need, want, or desire of another; and it is nice to be thanked for doing that well. The 'something broader' also relates to using your time and talent productively, and it is nice if the employer who purchases your time and directs the use of your talent expresses gratitude for your efforts.

THE CIVILIZED 'CITY' OF THE WORKPLACE

We are, all of us, social beings. We all know that the nice thing, the polite thing to do in any human interaction is to express gratitude whenever appropriate.

The word 'polite' derives from the Greek word for city, 'polis'. In a city – that is, in a civilized community – people are 'polite'. They are necessarily 'political', and they are governed by 'policies' that make life in the city more human, more livable. So it should be in the workplace.

Ingratitude signals a breakdown of politeness, leading to a depersonalisation of the normal politics of the workplace, and resulting in a situation where policies no longer represent guidelines for ordered behaviour, but fences to contain individual excesses. Any attempt to build a social order based on constraint is, ultimately, doomed to failure.

It can be argued that gratitude is a foundation for obligation. In an older vernacular, 'much obliged' was a way of saying 'thank you'. Not to thank another is, in effect, to regard oneself as unfettered by any obligation towards that other, free of even the basic social obligations of civility and courtesy.

CULTIVATING GRATITUDE IN YOUR OWN LIFE

If you are sensitive enough to notice the absence of gratitude in your workplace surroundings, and if you are personally (and perhaps deeply) wounded by ingratitude, the best remedy for your condition may also prove to be the beginning of a cure for the larger problem. Simply take it upon yourself to be very careful not to miss any opportunity to thank someone else – co-worker or customer, superior or subordinate, or anyone you meet in the workplace. Your courteous consideration, your civility, will become contagious. The gratitude you give, but may not yet have received, will eventually come back to you.

When this return of thanks begins to happen, your workplace will have begun to turn around. When gratitude becomes a habit, the workplace will be a more humane environment, a better place to be as well as a better place to work.

How many parents have said to their children over the years, 'What's the magic word?' That question comes at the opening of countless parent-child negotiations on any given day. The magic word is, of course, 'please'. Not far removed from that pleasant sound of politeness there is always an opportunity for an expression of gratitude. And this, of course, is not just for children. Civility and appropriate gratitude are important parts of any adult's identity as a social being. A thankless workplace diminishes those who work there.

Many years ago, I took a Sunday morning train from New York City to suburban White Plains for a visit with old friends. I knew they would be waiting at curbside so, when I arrived, I moved quickly down the platform, through the waiting room, and outside to the pick-up area. On the way through I noticed a hobo, a 'knight of the road', to whom I nodded and said hello. He followed me out of the station.

When I noticed him approaching me as I stood by the curb, I reached into my pocket for some coins. He waved me off declining the contribution and said, 'I just wanted to come out here and thank you. You're the first person who has said anything at all to me in two days'. That mumbled expression of gratitude for the elemental gift of human contact has stayed with me for years. How sad that both the contact and the thanks can be so rare in a person's transit through life.

Can anyone, anywhere, really believe there is nothing at all for which to say thanks?

Recently, I've noticed an interesting vocabulary development related to the way young Americans respond to expressions of thanks. It happened three times within an hour as I moved about on the Georgetown University campus; three times I heard, 'No problem', as the pleasant response to my expression of gratitude.

Someone held open a door; I said, 'Thanks' as I walked through and heard, 'No problem' in reply.

Someone else turned in an assignment at my desk and I said, 'Thank you'. 'No problem' was the immediate rejoinder.

Still another person delivered some good news by phone. 'Thanks for calling', I said, as we ended the conversation. 'No problem' were the words that went before the click of the receiver at the other end of the line.

Curious, isn't it, how 'you're welcome' has been lost somewhere in translation and is being replaced by a simple declaration of the absence of any problem? There is 'no problem' presumably, connected in any way with the transaction at hand. Nor is there any apparent problem anywhere on the immediate horizon. Or, could it be that this new usage has come into style because the young are now more in need of reassurance of freedom from problems than they were formerly in need of being made to feel welcome? Who can say?

I don't mean to suggest that too much should be read into this semantic shift. I'm just indulging in a playful juggling of words that have a way of changing all the time. Words come in and out of fashion without our noticing, but no one can fail to notice the absence of a word of thanks.

Familiar expressions of gratitude, unlike familiarity, have no potential whatever for breeding contempt. Unfamiliar expressions of gratitude will eventually catch on and find a place in the vernacular; I certainly have 'no problem' with that. And all of us will be 'much obliged' if the new expressions serve the cause of civility and courtesy by assuring a place for thanks in all circles of human interaction, not least in the workplace.

'Better open reproof than voiceless love', says the Book of Proverbs (27:5). Voiceless love is an issue that often needs attention in the family circle; voiceless thanks is a problem to be addressed in the world of work. Fortunately, anyone with a voice has all the equipment necessary to take that problem on.

CHAPTER NINE
BEING PASSED OVER

There is no single English word that catches the full sense of the workplace wound described in the phrase 'being passed over'.

'Forgotten' does not quite do it, because often the pass over is quite deliberate and fully conscious. Your higher-ups want to keep you where you are, or even drop you down a notch, or encourage you to go away. This can hurt.

'Jilted' is another nominee that fails to communicate the meaning of this workplace reality (although it seems to work well in explaining why some youthful romances fail). There is often more direct human contact in being jilted romantically than there is in being passed over in the workplace. A consultant friend told me of a manager he knows who remarked that he 'can handle headcount reduction' but just 'can't deal with firing people'. In other words, depersonalise the situation first, and then attend to the dirty work.

Many bosses prefer to walk right past the emotional ruins they know they are creating as they assign new responsibilities – promoting some subordinates while marooning or setting others adrift. We are all capable of walking over the lives and sensibilities of others and being quite oblivious to the damage we leave behind. The probability of that happening in civilized settings is reduced by virtue of the civility that is cultivated there. But cold, formal civility, with its separation of emotional attachments from workplace relationships, can encourage career passovers. Unlike the historic Passover that is preserved in Jewish memory and ritual, *workplace* pass overs feature no sense of rescue. They are often exquisitely lonely, painful affairs marked chiefly by a sense of profound abandonment.

Forget about the 'this-hurts-me-more-than-it-is-going-to-hurt-you' preamble; if directed at you, you won't even hear it. You may not hear anything but the news that someone else got the promotion. You have been passed over, so how should you react?

BEYOND THE REPLAY

I didn't deserve this. Why did this happen to me?

Repeated questions will propel your internal review of any workplace pass over; you will run play-by-play dissections of 'what happened and why'. The poet Samuel Hazo has a line I like: 'Can days of making sense/of days that make no sense/make sense?' Of course not. The anger roiling up within you will encourage you to play and replay reels of 'what-might-have-been' scenarios; 'if only' you had done this or that, or 'if only' someone else had done or not done something else. I can assure you of this: the replay phase, if you indulge it, will only sink you deeper into the quicksand of self-pity.

What, then, *should* you do? First give thanks for all the gifts you do possess, especially the talents that may at the moment be unnoticed or unappreciated by the higher-ups who passed you over. Subject your personal career assets – your knowledge, experience, education, skills, contacts, achievements, ideas – to careful review. This self-examination should focus first on how well you have used your assets. If you have not been using them well, you may find in this discovery an answer to the question of why you were passed over. (Do not, however, use the possibly valid explanation for your workplace pass over as an excuse to kick yourself around the block, to denigrate yourself endlessly.)

Review next the steps you took to let others see who you are, what you have done, and what you are capable of doing. You will recall that Jesus had some good advice about the relative position of lampstands and bushel baskets. Perhaps you have inadvertently kept your light hidden under a bushel basket and this is not only not doing you any good, but inflicting positive harm on your career. When that review is done, take more than a moment or two to trace the human relationships that are part of your working day. Leave aside, for the moment, questions of your own competence so that you can examine issues of interpersonal chemistry. How do you get along with others? Do others seem to perceive you as likable, pleasant to be around? Does your side of a typical conversation tend to focus on you or the other party? Is your learning curve a closed loop, or are you really open to the ideas of others? Is your workplace personality closed or open, supportive or suspicious, competitive or cooperative?

Once you've completed this review, it will help if you sit down with a few trusted friends to review your personal talent and skill inventory. Let them look at the scores you give yourself in your private self-assessment, and the reasons – as you have laid them out with all the objectivity you can muster – for this missed opportunity for an advance in your career. You will be both surprised and, yes, grateful to your friends at the end of such an exercise.

THE 'BAD BOSS'

I know a person who was treated shabbily by a 'bad boss'. My friend is now convinced that such a problem can, in fact, become a significant career advantage. 'Bad bosses can make your career. It gets so bad that you quit, and before you know it, you find yourself in a better job!'

If you (with some help from your trusted friends) conclude that your experience of being passed over relates to problems that are proper to your boss, not to you, that knowledge may well open up for you a new door to a better future.

ON ADVANCING

There are also persons whose 'ambition' for advancement is driven by the expectations of others. When such a person is passed over, the reaction can be a complicated by criticism, even scorn, from those whose expectations have raised the bar higher than the affected individual ever really wanted to jump.

Dr David Morrison describes the case of an executive he calls Tom. Tom's wife, Anne, came from a family of uniformly high achievers in the male ranks. She put constant and heavy pressure on Tom to succeed. He was motivated more by her expectations than any other drive. In effect, Tom was working for his wife, not his employer.

On the job, he succeeded in building a reputation for pushiness and excessive risk-taking. His insatiable appetite for recognition (recognition he could 'bring home' for his wife to 'see') alienated everyone else in the workplace.

Tom was thoroughly disliked. His focus on upward advancement at any and all costs led him to ignore opportunities for cultivating his own competence and pursuing his genuine interests.

Since work, in and of itself, had no meaning for Tom, it provided no basis for personal gratification – except as a fulcrum for status and an anchor for marital stability. Consequently, Tom did not work well with others. Any 'success' that came to him worked against the best interests of the company.

It is no wonder that persons like Tom will eventually be passed over because, in Morrison's words, 'They will provoke cynicism and distrust when they push others to be concerned about quality or commitment to the organisation. Their own true values will be communicated by their behaviour and mixed messages. As they focus on short-term gains on their way up the corporate ladder, others will have to clean up the longer-term consequences of their actions.' I call the syndrome from which Tom suffers *career tyranny*.

Career tyranny relates to expectations. It can be imposed on you by the expectations of others or by the unrealistic promises you make to yourself. Those who are disinclined towards self-examination are particularly vulnerable. Honest self-assessment is absolutely necessary to deal productively with a workplace pass over. At the point of pass over – a crisis for any sensitive human being – the self-assessment trigger must be pulled. If you've been wronged, your spirituality will see you through. If you are wrong and they are right, your spirituality, especially its Pauline dimensions of patience, faithfulness and self-control, will put a platform under you to support you in the setback and in your push-off towards the next realistic opportunity for advancement. In the process, you will find yourself giving humility a good name!

WHAT WE DO, WHAT WE ARE

Being passed over is not as bad as being laid off, of course, but it can cause some of the same kind of psychological damage. Regrettably, too many of us are psychologically conditioned to believing that what we do is what we are. When we are doing nothing (as a consequence, for instance, of being fired or laid off), we falsely and unfortunately conclude that we *are* nothing. Similarly, when we are passed over in the workplace, we tend to conclude that we have nowhere to go but down or out. Simply staying in place where you are – marking time, letting the clock run out – is a sign of failure.

Simply *being* is not enough to support one's self-esteem. One must *do* more and more. And the *doing* has to keep rising to new levels of achievement, compensation, and prestige if it is to sustain one's sense of self-worth.

This approach to life and work is not just dangerous; it is crazy. You are, after all, a human being, not a human doing! You have to come to terms with that simple truth when reversals shake your self-confidence.

You should be able to draw reassurance on this point from that bank account your spirituality provides. If you can't, something of extraordinary value has not yet been deposited there. It is, after all, a question of value – your bedrock, non-negotiable values – that is at stake when you struggle with the doing-versus-being problem. If there is no answer from within when you seek reassurance on who you are and what you're worth, your inner account is missing a very fundamental value: the unshakable conviction that you are a unique person, regardless of what you do, and that you belong to a personal, knowing, loving, caring and all-powerful God who can never be anything but faithful to you. God holds your destiny in his hands.

FAITH OR FATALISM

Several years ago, I learned a lot from a fifty-one-year-old unemployed marketing executive who says he had decided it was time to leave his job with a major pharmaceutical company. Here is just one paragraph from a five-page letter he sent me two years into an, as then, not yet successful job search:

> Unemployment has had a positive effect on my life in that it has made me a much more sensitive and caring person. I have been humbled and that is good. Last year for a time I was driving an airport limousine to make twenty dollars a trip (every little bit helps). On one occasion I picked up one of my former peers who still works at my last company. That was humbling! I keep telling myself that some day I will find financial security and I will look back with gratitude for having had the chance to become a better person. I remain hopeful, but my trust is only in my own effort. I expect no help and want (and deserve) no sympathy. My situation is the result of the choices I personally made. I have no one to be angry at, including myself. I am proud of my strength but I do fear despair.

I am happy to report that he never lost hope and that he toughed it out for two more years before reconnecting with full-time, satisfying employment. In the same letter, he disclosed to me that he found no 'comfort or nourishment from religious faith although I confess that I have occasionally asked for God's help, but always with the expressed thought that "if you are listening", or "just in case you hear me". If I am wrong, and God does intervene selectively, my lack of conviction dooms me. I do believe in God, but I do not know him or understand him. He is not personal, so there is no reason to be angry with him.'

Those sad words left me pondering what his outlook would be like if he had only caught the Pauline value of faithfulness and let it go to work within him.

Without faith, scripture is an unlighted torch and spiritual guidelines cannot help because it takes the spark of faith to activate them.

The gift of faith is available to anyone who decides to take it. Remember this whenever you are passed over (or confronted by something worse). Let faith go to work for you. It will surely make a difference. Meanwhile, search within for the faith to say 'Amen' to these ancient words from the Book of Wisdom (15:1-3):

> But you, our God, are good and true,
>   slow to anger, and governing all with mercy.
> For even if we sin, we are yours, and know your might;
>   but we will not sin, knowing that we belong to you.
> For to know you well is complete justice,
>   and to know your might is the root of immortality.

CHAPTER TEN
LAYOFF

Anyone who has been through it will tell you that a layoff is a kind of death. Typically, news of the layoff will be broken (usually awkwardly) in the workplace, but the wound inflicted by that news is nursed at home. The vocabulary of job loss says you are 'out of work', 'beached', 'streeted', 'on the bricks', but you are usually hiding out at home. You are trying to find your way back into some workplace somewhere, yet, all too often you are on your own and lonely, hopeful of plugging your wound with a good job before the lifeblood of your self-esteem drains all the way out.

Right up there next to death and divorce, and on equal status with cancer or cardiac arrest, you will find mid-career job loss on anyone's list of stress-producing personal reversals.

The familiar expression 'I could write a book' is doubly applicable here. This reflection on layoffs could easily take on book-length proportions. And I did, in fact, write a book about the experiences of 150 men and women who were separated from their jobs in the wake of corporate downsizing. It was published by Adams (Holbrook, MA) in 1995 under the title *Finding Work without Losing Heart: Bouncing Back from Mid-Career Job Loss*. That book is now out of print but available free online at: http://www.sju.edu/academics/hsb/resources/finding work/index.html.

As part of the research that resulted in that publication, I learned that some discouraged job seekers found comfort in the psalms. So to make the psalter more available and user-friendly for Christians and Jews who are struggling with the stress of unemployment, I edited a prayer book of psalms for discouraged job seekers. It was published by Sheed & Ward (Kansas City, Missouri) in 1995 as *Take Courage: Psalms of*

Support and Encouragement. Regrettably, it is now out of print, but the psalms, of course, are not. They are available for use on a psalm-a-day basis by those who are struggling with both their faith and their job search. From the psalter, you may wish to select encouraging phrases that can give voice to your needs and feelings as you begin the new job of reconnecting with meaningful employment.

But you, Lord, are a shield around me. (Psalm 3:4)

Restore again our fortunes, Lord. (Psalm 126:4)

And now, Lord, what future do I have?
You are my only hope. (Psalm 39:8)

You are my help and deliverer.
Lord, do not delay! (Psalm 70:6)

Show me the path I should walk,
for to you I entrust my life. (Psalm 143:8)

RELIGIOUS FAITH AND PHYSICAL AND MENTAL HEALTH

Some years ago at the annual meeting of the American Association for the Advancement of Science, Dr Dale A. Matthews, of the Georgetown University Medical Centre, reported on the outcome of a study he and others conducted on the relationship of religion to health. In three-fourths of the 212 cases they studied, the researchers found a positive effect of religious commitment on health. It proved to be helpful in dealing with drug abuse, alcoholism, depression, cancer, high blood pressure, and heart disease. Dr Harold G. Koenig, of Duke University Medical Centre, reported that 'people who attend church are both physically healthier and less depressed'.

Precisely how religion works to make people healthier is not at all clear, but the studies can at least serve to encourage anyone who is so inclined to let religion and spirituality shore up their sinking spirits and offset the discouragement, and occasional depression, associated with the typical job search.

If you are out of work, you have to realise that you have a self to serve during your transition to your next job. You are your sole client, your chief concern. As I put it in my book *Finding Work without Losing Heart*:

> Throughout the transition, you are the centre of a process of personal self-assessment and self-renewal; you must be or become the object of your own self-esteem and self-respect. You are the one who has to guard against self-pity and loss of self-confidence. You are the agent of change. If you are to find new employment, you have to take the initiative. The process is fundamentally self-serving, and there is absolutely nothing to apologise for in acknowledging that it is. Ultimately, the job search is a test of character. And character, as both history and literature attest, is proved in action.

During counselling sessions, I've often said to individual job seekers, 'Your job search is your character in motion'. If spirituality is, as it should be, part of your character, you can expect your spirituality, your prayer elevated to a lifestyle, to work for you during this transition.

CHARACTER AND FAITH
You will no doubt find yourself frustrated and tense from time to time because you are not 'in control' of your employment destiny. Dependent, as your faith tells you that you always are, on the sustaining grace of your creator-God, you have to wonder how you ever got the idea that you were independently 'in control' in those glory days when you were fully employed.

Perhaps, like many others who have encountered personal or career reversals, you have convinced yourself that the Book of Job has your name on it. Yet it would be a misreading of Job (and a disservice to yourself) to blame God. Reflect on these words from the Introduction to the Book of Job in The Jerusalem

Bible: 'In his anguish [Job] reaches out for God; God eludes him, but Job still trusts in his goodness ... This is the book's lesson: faith must remain even when understanding fails.' The faith that remains will have you trusting in and reaching out for God. That is spirituality at work.

One job seeker, who came to me for help as I was writing this book, told me that he had been laid off several times over the years. Earlier in his career, he returned to the US after working overseas for an international relief agency where, as administrator of the feeding programmes in an impoverished part of the world, he had been 'handling millions of pounds of foodstuffs every year'. He thought, he said, that with his experience it would be easy to find a challenging job back in Washington, DC. He was wrong. He found himself 'chronically unemployed, on welfare, and reduced to using food stamps'. One day, someone from his parish community, whom he did not know at all well, appeared on his doorstep to present him with four bags of groceries and $50. 'I just thought', the benefactor said, 'that you might appreciate a little help.'

The beneficiary of this gift, reflecting on the event years later, told me how he had been struck at the time with the irony of the situation. He was a person who, when employed, had given away millions of dollars worth of food, and now he found himself unemployed and on the receiving end of food relief. He also recalled for me how hard it was for him to accept help. 'We don't accept things easily,' he said; 'we think we always have to reciprocate.'

To his credit, he recognised this for what it was – a spiritual problem relating to false pride and an exaggerated sense of independence. False pride and an exaggerated sense of self-reliance have to be dealt with immediately upon separation from a job. This does not mean that you should demean yourself in preparation for encounters with potential employers. Far from it! It does mean, however, that it is going to take a lot of humility to get yourself back in gear and on the road to re-employment.

HANDLING THE BAD NEWS

A consulting firm I know of is hired by major corporations to train corporate executives in the 'art of laying people off': what to do and what not to do in breaking the bad news. After a manager, appropriately trained, fires a person, that person is taken, along with other displaced employees, to a room where a counsellor from this firm is there to help.

John Fontana, who once did this kind of work, recalled for me a day when he was the consultant in a room with about a dozen managers who had just received the bad news. There was shocked disbelief. Tears flowed freely. One woman, who had been through it twice before in her career, offered the hopeful observation that after each of her previous layoffs, she found a better job. Another refugee to the 'crying room', a thirty-something gentleman who always had ambitions of becoming a comedian, attempted to lighten the atmosphere by asking the others to imagine that they had a gun with just two bullets and found themselves in a room with three others – two notorious human rights violators (he named two well-known dictators) and their own CEO (also mentioned by name), who had just made the downsizing decision. 'What would you do?' After a pause, he answered his own question: 'You would, of course, shoot the CEO twice!' Their laughter encouraged the would-be comedian to begin his new career right there. He told more jokes and the whole group got into it as they all went out to lunch together.

PATIENCE

Laughter belongs in the medicine cabinet of anyone who has to deal with the terrible pain a layoff inevitably brings. But job loss is, of course, no laughing matter, in either the short- or long-term view of things. The only satisfying solution to a mid-career layoff is a 360-degree turnaround back to meaningful employment. You have to make that happen through persistence, prayer, and, yes, some laughs, through a search process of uncertain endurance that will surely test one of those nine Pauline Criteria that you may not regard as part of your strong suit: the virtue of patience. Your spirituality can make a virtue out of patient persistence; it can put patience to work for you in your campaign to return to work.

Patience shows total respect for the facts. Romano Guardini called it 'the deepest possible acceptance of things as they are'. This is not to suggest that things cannot change. It simply acknowledges that it takes time to produce more favourable circumstances.

Your impatience is a protest against the facts; your patience is a tacit commitment to participate in a process that will overcome unfavorable facts. Recall again *Othello* (Act II, Scene iii): 'How poor are they that have not patience!/What wound did ever heal but by degrees?' The wound of layoff is no exception to this rule.

CHAPTER ELEVEN
PREJUDICE

Samuel DeWitt Proctor, a distinguished American educator who served, during his long academic career, as president of Virginia Union University and North Carolina A&T, and also held professorships at Duke and Rutgers, was born into a middle-class African-American family in 1921. 'My daddy would go to work everyday', he once recalled, 'around white people who treated him like he was a boy. But when he came home at 4 o'clock, he would practice his violin, go to his Masonic meetings and church meetings, and he was a new person. He taught us this kind of transcendence: the ability to rise above whatever people thought or said about us.'

The Substance of Things Hoped For is the title, borrowed from the Letter to the Hebrews, of Proctor's fine 1996 book written to inspire young black people whom he urges 'to give up the paralysis of analysis and feelings of hopelessness'. Proctor's grandmother, once a slave, earned a degree from Hampton University in 1882. Of her he recalls: 'My grandmother was born into slavery, but I never once heard her say anything evil about anyone. That's how they got by then. It wasn't escapism, as some would say today. That was faith.' This kind of faith, embodied in the seventh Pauline value, is a firm foundation for a functioning spirituality, and is *all* the protection you need when prejudice strikes in the workplace.

PREJUDICE: A CONTEMPORARY REALITY
Prejudice is evident just about everywhere. It is targeted singly or in combination of race, religion, ethnicity, accent, national origin, sex and sexual orientation, age, disability, educational and economic status (regardless of whether that status is perceived as too high or too low). Prejudice is irrational. Pre-

judgement – the essence of *pre-judice* – is an exercise of deliberate, calculated shutdown, usually triggered solely by external appearances. Based exclusively on characteristics like those just listed, and others not catalogued here, abilities and motives are attributed to persons without any regard for objective truth. Prejudice reflects an arrogant conviction that the targeted person would be 'better' if he or she were exactly like the one making the pre-judgement!

What if you are the target of another's prejudice? Well, begin by acknowledging that you can never *make* someone like you. You look foolish when you try. Distinct personal likes and dislikes are normal and universal. Chances are you will be more likeable in the eyes of most of the people with whom you interact if you successfully assimilate the nine Pauline Criteria within the core of your personality. Once possessed, these values will not only support you but also show through to others. And yet there will *always* be some who, without prejudice, simply won't like you.

You can reasonably hope that these people won't hate you or do you any harm; you can be happy and productive even though you don't win their vote. And you can easily overcome the adolescent impulse to think life not worth living simply because you do not receive universal affection and approval. Moving on in the face of this kind of reality is what it means to be a mature and emotionally well-balanced person. But the question remains: how do you deal with prejudice?

Many of the workplace wounds discussed in earlier chapters originate in prejudice. Because of prejudice, you might experience criticism, betrayal, false accusations and a host of other problems. In dealing with those problems along lines suggested in this book, you are, of course, dealing with prejudice. But the point to be made here, in this brief consideration of prejudice itself, is that only a functioning spirituality will help you, as an individual, transcend – literally and effectively rise above – the age-old problem of prejudice.

There are legal remedies to the problem of prejudice that can and should be pursued by individuals. There are tools and tactics of confrontation, and strategies of organisation and negotiation, that are better employed by groups than by individual victims of prejudice. Some victims are provoked to violence singly or in mobs; there is no room for that, of course, in a nine-point programme that includes 'gentleness' and 'self-control'.

Non-violence is, in the metaphor I used earlier, a slingshot strategy that can overcome prejudice. It can reinforce your personal stand against prejudice. The believer simply has to believe that love, joy, peace, patience, kindness, generosity, faithfulness, gentleness, and self-control are pillars of strength against the crushing potential of prejudice. When prejudice threatens to get you down, these values will lift you up. And that is the meaning of transcendence. You can rise above it all.

Consider once again the words Samuel Proctor wrote about his grandmother: 'I never once heard her say anything evil about anyone. That's how they got by then. It wasn't escapism, as some would say today. That was faith.' But often that won't be enough.

CAN YOU FEEL IT? CAN YOU TRANSCEND IT?

Imagine yourself to be the target of flat-out, hands-down prejudice, the kind of prejudice African-Americans experience in the housing markets, the kind that women in business bump up against when they hit the so-called glass ceiling. Would you be able to summon up the spiritual resources to meet the challenge without sacrificing your own principles and diminishing your own integrity?

If you have never had any real experience of prejudice, try this classic experiment: do a simple role play in a circle of friends where, for example, blue-eyed people are arbitrarily designated as inferior. Their rights can be violated with impunity. They are denied equal access to facilities. They are just walked over by those whose eyes are brown, or green, or anything but blue. Play that game for more than a few minutes, even among friends, and your blue eyes will soon be seeing red!

I would argue to the end that, for the preservation of your own humanity, you, like Samuel Proctor's grandmother, must never say anything evil about the person or persons behind the prejudice. I would also argue, however, that you should speak out in truth against the injustice and speak up without apology for your rights. (First, however, be sure to filter that speech through the Pauline Criteria for assurance that it is the Spirit speaking from within you!) Remember that, in the workplace, *how* you speak up will be important; style can be supportive or destructive of the substance you feel compelled to communicate.

INSIDE ANOTHER'S SKIN

Harper Lee's *To Kill a Mockingbird* is a great novel about prejudice, the struggle for justice, and the unfolding awareness of these realities in the mind of a child. As if to prepare the reader for what is to come later in the story, and as he is preparing his child for life, the lawyer-father Atticus has a chat with his six-year-old daughter Scout, who has just announced, at the end of her first day in school, that she will not return to school. Her unenlightened first-grade teacher, the reader discovers, told her that morning that she would have to unlearn the reading skills already learned in the lap of her father (where, the now adult daughter-narrator recalls, 'reading was something that just came to me. … I could not remember when the lines above Atticus' moving finger separated into words, but I had stared at them all the evenings in my memory'). Her father now patiently explains a lesson that all of us have trouble putting into practice:

> 'First of all,' he said, 'if you can learn a simple trick, Scout, you'll get along a lot better with all kinds of folks. You never really understand a person until you consider things from his point of view – '
> 'Sir?'
> '– until you climb into his skin and walk around in it.'

So that's the first thing any one of us has to do, even in the midst of hurt and the heat of anger. Try to climb inside the skin of the person who is harming you to see the world from his or her perspective (even though, in the case of prejudice, you will find it to be a distorted view). As I indicated, prejudice is, by definition, a pre-judgement. That mind was already made up. What is blocking the vision? What might you be doing to prevent those other eyes from opening or, if open, seeing clearly?

If you walk around inside the skin of another for a while, it will affect your style of reaction; you might begin to see that person's problem and then be better able to figure out your own next best step. This is not to suggest that you were somehow wrong and that you can now make a return trip 'to your senses'. Not at all! It simply means that by allowing yourself to think for a moment as the other person thinks, you might get a better handle on the problem to be solved. It also increases the probability that you will be more inclined to treat the person or persons behind that problem as you would treat yourself.

I mentioned this exchange between Atticus and his daughter Scout to former Pennsylvania governor Robert P. Casey, while he was still in office and recovering from the life-saving surgery that transplanted a liver and heart from a black man's body into his own. He had read *To Kill a Mockingbird* many years before, and noted with appreciation that some well-wisher had given him another copy while he was recuperating from the transplant surgery.

'You didn't climb inside your donor's skin,' I said; 'his organs were transplanted into yours. Does that have any effect at all now on your view of race relations?'

'It sure does', he replied.

And Mrs Casey told me how, a few months after the surgery, when everyone across the state knew that the governor was doing well, an African-American woman who was a total stranger greeted her warmly in a Philadelphia department store, expressed her joy at the governor's progress, then added: 'And we're so glad we were able to help!'

The governor, always on the side of victims of racial injustice, intensified his efforts during his remaining years in office to reduce both the unemployment and drug traffic that set the stage for his donor's death by gun shot in an economically depressed western Pennsylvania town. Casey later worked on the establishment of an endowment that would memorialise his benefactor by financing medical education for young blacks who want to become transplant surgeons. Robert Casey was, of course, dealing with disease, not prejudice. But the origin of the gift of life that enabled him to cope continued to motivate him – from within – to help victims of discrimination.

It is unlikely that you will have transplanted organs to motivate you from within, but they will not be necessary. There can be an internalised spirituality driving you to 'do the right thing' and setting the boundaries for appropriate action. If you are a Christian, the pattern and style of your reaction to prejudice has to be influenced by words that you might not always be anxious to hear: 'But to you who hear I say, love your enemies, do good to those who hate you, bless those who curse you, pray for those who mistreat you.' If you have the courage to read on, you can pick up the lesson in the Gospel of Luke, chapter 6, at verse 29.

Walk around for a while inside the skin of a prejudiced person, in or out of the workplace, and you will find evidence of all the weapons you should never use to fight prejudice: hatred, pettiness, fear, spite, ignorance. Apparently, Samuel DeWitt Proctor's grandmother recognised in her wisdom that these were not only unworthy of her, but that they would surely be ineffective in the defence of her dignity. She had faith. So do you.

Use your faith-based resourcefulness to speak the truth in love. Act firmly and fairly to get those scales of justice back in balance. If you lose your poise in the struggle for justice, you may kill your chances of ever winning your rights. You will also have lost sight of the values that define your better self, and that would amount to handing over to prejudice a victory it should never have.

Let the word of God, spoken through the prophet Amos, sink into your soul to be lifted up into consciousness whenever you are feeling the burden of prejudice:

Seek good and not evil,
   that you may live;
Then truly will the Lord, the God of hosts,
   be with you as you claim!
Hate evil and love good,
   and let justice prevail at the gate ...
let justice surge like water,
   and goodness like an unfailing stream. (5:14, 24)

The rules of spirituality are simple and direct. Resist any impulse to return evil for evil. Go for the good, even when evil is inflicted on you. Go for the good and justice will prevail!

CHAPTER TWELVE
SEXUAL HARASSMENT

There is no need to take today's newspaper story on sexual harassment as a point of departure for a discussion of the subject. There will surely be another story tomorrow, and the day after tomorrow, and presumably on the day you find yourself reading this book; by then today's story will be long gone (although not, it is fair to assume, completely forgotten).

I begin, then, with the presumption that you know, at least on an instinctive level, what sexual harassment is; that you may not be completely familiar with all the legal decisions on this issue; and that you yourself are not a candidate for initiating this kind of activity ('self-control' is, after all, one of the personal principles of spirituality you are assimilating). You may well, however, find yourself some day on the receiving end of sexual harassment.

Western democracies tend to define sexual harassment in these or similar terms:

> Unwelcome sexual advances, requests for sexual favours, and other verbal or physical conduct of a sexual nature constitute sexual harassment when submission to or rejection of this conduct explicitly or implicitly affects an individual's employment, unreasonably interferes with an individual's work performance, or creates an intimidating, hostile, or offensive work environment.

We all understand that the workplace is not populated by angels or disembodied spirits; it is inhabited by sexual beings with instincts and appetites that can, of course, be controlled. Indeed, they must be controlled if human dignity is to be preserved in the workplace.

Sexual *attraction* will presumably be at work in the typical workplace every day; sexual *activity* is an altogether separate issue. Attraction becomes harassment when it prompts conduct that, whether rejected or submitted to, affects employment status, impairs work performance, and produces an intimidating, hostile, or offensive work environment.

WHAT TO DO
Many men and women (typically, more women than men) have good reason to complain of harassment, but many more work in intimidating, hostile and offensive work environments where the reasons for those uncomfortable conditions have nothing to do with sex. Cases have to be considered on their merits, and the presumption of a sexual motivation behind unwelcome conduct always has to be examined carefully. But what if it happens to *you*, and what if you know you are innocent and *this* is sexual harassment?

WHAT DO YOU DO?
Register your disapproval immediately; let the harasser know that this is unwanted and unacceptable. By openly registering your reaction, you make it absolutely clear to the harasser that the moves are in fact unwelcome, so it's best to be quite direct. Direct does not mean aggressive; registering disapproval only takes a word and a well-defined 'stop' gesture.

It is unwise to enter into a protracted discussion about what you will or will not accept, about what might or might not be appropriate on the job. Make it unambiguously clear that you reject non-professional advances; then see what happens. If the person who caused the problem has any sense, that will be the end of the matter.

If the behaviour recurs, of if you have a sense that your silence would lead to the victimisation of others, you should take the one-step-up approach and report the matter to a superior – preferably to the harasser's superior, but certainly to your own. In the immediate aftermath of any incident, you should also reflect on your own behaviour as you run through your nine-point checklist in the evening and early morning. You will want to make sure that neither your signals nor your motives were mixed in any exchanges that could have led up to the unwelcome event.

'THE WORLD'

Sexual harassment is almost always part of a power game and because it is, I want to use this occasion to discuss a spiritual matter that goes by the name of the 'triple concupiscence'.

If that word sounds strange, take it apart. You hear Valentine's Day references to Cupid. You know what cupidity means (and you hate to see it in anyone because it carries desire across the line to possessiveness and avarice). The prefix 'con' simply means 'with', so 'concupiscence' just means 'with desire'. More often than not it is taken to refer to lust, or ardent sexual desire. The triple concupiscence is the lust of the flesh, the lust of the eye, and the lust for power over other persons.

This is all part of human nature. Any normal, healthy person will recognise stirrings within that reflect a desire, rooted in one's human nature, for sexual union, possession of things that attract the eye, and for power over others. These impulses, of course, have to be contained, dealt with responsibly, but there is no point in trying to deny that they exist.

In the First Letter of John (2:15-17) the scriptural basis for reflection on this triple concupiscence is presented:

> Do not love the world or the things of the world. If anyone loves the world, the love of the Father is not in him. For all that is in the world, sensual lust, enticements for the eyes, and a pretentious life, is not from the Father but is from the world. Yet the world and its enticements are passing away. But whoever does the will of God remains forever.

John's use of the term 'world' here requires some explanation. The word is meant here to signify all that is not of God. Elsewhere – for instance in the Gospel of John (3:16) – the word 'world' appears in a more positive sense:

For God so loved the world that he gave his only Son, so that everyone who believes in him might not perish but might have eternal life. For God did not send his Son into the world to condemn the world, but that the world might be saved through him.

Throughout scripture, 'the world' is viewed as good, as lovable, worth saving, worth working in, worth transforming. In the quotation from 1 John 2:15-17, where John warns the believer to be wary of the pull of these three drives that are so familiar to human nature, John wants the believer to do God's will and thus live forever with God, rather than letting natural appetites, these desires for 'passing' things, run wild and pull him or her away from God.

Another widely used translation of this set of three drives is: 'Carnal allurements, enticements for the eye, the life of empty show'. Sexual harassment directly relates, of course, to the first. The advertising industry plays on the second (and, in the process, reinforces selfish values that encourage sexual harassment). And the 'life of empty show' or the 'pretentious life' refers to a state of mind characterised by pride and the desire to dominate.

This, then, is the arena that catches up all those 'Interest-Excitement' values, the power plays, and the drive for prestige that constitute the 'world's' way of measuring success. These are not the values that respect human dignity and foster the Pauline value of self-control. Rather, they are 'dis-values' that your spirituality is meant to overcome.

You could easily name nine (and possibly ninety-nine) 'worldly' values like fame, fortune, and power that run directly counter to the nine Pauline pillars that can uphold your human nature for the long haul into eternal happiness. Virtually all the false values on that list will be supportive of the selfishness that defines the sexual harasser.

APPROACHING OTHERS WITH YOUR PROBLEM
If you are employed in a place that has no sexual harassment policy, you have work to do. Don't wait for an unwelcome

event to occur; find out why there is no policy and when there's going to be one. If your employer has a policy, examine it for completeness and inquire about enforcement. Are accusations made public? It is understandable why they might not be. Are documented adverse findings against an accused harasser a matter of public record within the company? They should be. The time-tested principle of 'punish with pitiless publicity' (even without the assistance of billboards and headlines), when applied to genuine offenders, works wonders in the discouragement of sexual harassment.

Included in a useful and strong workplace policy would be: (1) physical assaults of a sexual nature; (2) unwanted sexual advances, propositions or other sexual comments; (3) sexual or discriminatory displays or publications anywhere in the workplace; and (4) retaliation for sexual harassment complaints.

If you look to scripture for some spiritual principle that would be helpful in the context of sexual harassment, you are likely to find yourself with the Book of Daniel, chapter 13, where you will find the famous story of Susanna – a passage some have referred to as the first detective story!

Susanna was the wife of Joakim and the target of the lustful desire of two 'elders', who were also judges in the Babylonian community. They trapped Susanna in the garden of her home where they had hidden to observe her bathing. They threatened to accuse her of adultery with a young man unless she submitted to their desires. She refused, was brought to trial on the next day, and condemned to death.

> But Susanna cried aloud: 'O Eternal God, you know what is hidden and are aware of all things before they come to be: you know that they have testified falsely against me. Here I am about to die, though I have done none of the things with which these wicked men have charged me.'
>
> The Lord heard her prayer. As she was being led to execution, God stirred up the holy spirit of a young boy named Daniel ... (13:42-45)

And Daniel came to her defence. He chided the Israelites for condemning her 'without examination and without clear evidence'. Back to court they went. Daniel separated the two elders so that he could question them individually about their charge that Susanna had dismissed her maids from the garden so that she could be alone there with an unnamed young man.

'Now, then, if you were a witness,' said Daniel to the first of the two elders, 'tell me under what tree you saw them together.' 'Under a mastic tree', he replied. And to the second elder Daniel put the same question: 'Tell me under what tree you surprised them.' 'Under an oak', he answered. Daniel's response to each was the same: 'Your fine lie has cost you your head.' So the judges were themselves judged; the two elders were sentenced to death. 'The whole assembly cried aloud, blessing God who saves those that hope in him. They rose up against the two elders, for by their own words Daniel had convicted them of perjury. According to the law of Moses, they inflicted on them the penalty they had plotted to impose on their neighbor' (60-61).

This wisdom principle, rooted in the Bible, assures the believer that innocence will be defended and malice punished. The believer knows that God 'saves those that hope in him' (Daniel 13:60), as happened in the story of Susanna. This belief is, of course, underscored by the Pauline principle of faithfulness.

The reader of 1 John 2:15-17 receives fair warning against the lust (understood as uncontrolled desire) of the flesh, the eyes, and the drive to dominate. So deposit these inspired bits of wisdom into your spirituality account now, reflect on them often, and peg them to that ninth Pauline guideline: the principle of self-control.

Knowing your own human nature well enough to admit that you have the capacity for harassment and other excesses can work to your advantage. That knowledge can serve as a very effective defence against excesses, including harassment, that could come your way from others who, unlike you, may be out of control.

CHAPTER THIRTEEN
MISTAKES

'Nobody knows the trouble I've seen.' Review your mistakes, and you may be tempted to indulge the impulse to feel sorry for yourself, and sing along in the words of this old saying. You'll find comfort in those words only if you believe that everyone else but you lives in an all-win, never-lose world.

Whether or not you have reconciled yourself to the fact that the 'old rockin' chair' may eventually get you, you should nevertheless come to terms right now with the stark fact that the human condition has, in fact, had you all along – right from the beginning.

Mistakes often seem pointless; they tend to reflect Linda Pastan's poetic salute to a workout on a stationary bicycle:

… this ride feels
much like life itself – going nowhere
strenuously.

In time, though, most of us are willing to concede that even though you may feel put upon at times, progress is possible and most mistakes can be repaired. Mistakes and reversals are bound to happen. There is no win-win world for everyone all the time.

Physically, unless you are quite young, you've been wearing out for years. Intellectually, you are probably active and alert, although you know that you can let yourself 'peak before your time' by just not attending to intellectual exercises – not using your mind. Psychologically, you can grow stronger every day, just so long as the physical house that holds your psychological furniture keeps standing. Of course, you may be one who suffered a severe setback before you were old enough to know what was happening to you: a congenital defect, an inherited disease, an accident in infancy, a reversal explainable simply in terms of your location in the human condition.

It will happen sooner or later. From the start, an army of 'Ds' is arrayed against you and all those with whom you share the human condition: disappointment, discouragement, disease, defeat. Not all at once, nor all the time, nor to the same degree, but each of those 'Ds' will touch you sometime. Eventually and inevitably, the Big D – death – will see that you shed your 'mortal coil'. Neither you nor anyone else likes to think about that. But there it is: the human condition with its unavoidable end to your pursuit of happiness. That end, however, is just the beginning, your faith assures you, of a happiness that will never end. And you have to *believe* (especially when you are reeling from a recent setback) that all the happiness you have already known, and will continue to enjoy here on earth, can serve to summon up some faint idea of how great eternal happiness will be.

THE ALTERNATIVE

I'm always amused when, inquiring about someone's progress in recovering from serious surgery or a near-fatal accident, I receive a half-smile and the reply, 'I'm doing rather well thanks, considering the alternative!' Does it take an automobile accident or serious illness to make us take some time to consider, with the eye of faith, that great alternative? There is the story about the two elderly friends who died weeks apart and met again in heaven. One said to the other, 'If I had known it was going to be like this, I would never have eaten all that oat bran!'

I do not intend to try to set forth in words what you can expect to find in the hereafter. That reality is something that 'eye has not seen, and ear has not heard' (1 Corinthians 2:9). I aim, instead, to help you learn to address, from a faith perspective, the terrible reality of here-and-now reversals: physical, intellectual, psychological, financial. Why pain? Why suffering? Why me? In these pages, I want to walk you through a reflective survey of the ground that could go out from under you, sometimes through your own fault by virtue of your own mistakes, at any stage of your journey through life and work. Mistakes are an unavoidable part of life. That's reality.

It's true: just about anything can go wrong at any time. The legendary Murphy put that into some kind of 'law' that you may have had occasion to cite in the past and are likely to repeat in the future.

You don't have to be paranoid to realise that oppositional forces are arrayed against you. Not only will you make your fair share (or more) of mistakes, you already know full well that traps and pitfalls are somehow 'out there', waiting for you. They are very much part of what you have to deal with in the down-to-earth reality of daily life in any workplace. These traps have the potential to pull you down, or they can occasion your overcoming the obstacles that you find in your path.

You really are going to have to deal with personal reversals that are neither work-defined nor necessarily work-occasioned; they do, however, have direct effects on how you manage to do what you are called to do in the workplace. What follows is intended to help you cover that terrain and to keep your eye on the prize when the awareness of your mistakes weighs you down.

COURAGE

Courage is not an explicitly stated element in the set of Pauline Criteria that define a Christian spirituality and give evidence of the presence of the Holy Spirit within the soul of the believer. Explicit or not, however, courage is included in the category of love, and it is surely part of the spirituality you want to have for your journey through life.

There is no reversal that cannot be met with courage. Courage is grace ('grace under pressure', in Ernest Hemingway's words). Courage is strength, strength you don't even know you have (and, without faith, would not have). Courage is your grip on the 'slingshot' spirituality that will enable you to hold your own and more against any reversal, even one of Goliath-like proportions. Courage, finally, is the ability to face up to your mistakes and move on in spite of them.

FORGIVENESS

'I made a mistake once,' the comedian's storyline goes; 'I acknowledged making an error and later discovered that I was wrong.' Not so with the rest of the human community. We all make mistakes and most of us have difficulty admitting it.

Mistakes can be honest, hasty, stupid, expensive, careless, critical, big or small, private or quite public. Are they always forgivable? They certainly should be, at least in the sense of self-forgiveness on the part of the one who makes them.

If you cannot forgive yourself, you raise a wall against forgiveness coming your way from anyone else. There are times when the consequences of a mistake will cost you a friend, some money, your job, reputation, or possibly your life. Even so, no mistake is beyond forgiveness. Nor are second starts for you ever foreclosed, as long as you live. The mistake may have removed you from the situation where you once lived or worked, but you can – and must –learn from the experience, and move ahead in the hope that those who knew you in that place and at that time can forgive you and still think well of you.

ADMITTING MISTAKES

A functioning spirituality will give you the clarity and the courage to admit your mistakes and move on.

You don't have to take a full-page ad in the newspaper to tell the world how and why you erred. You simply have to hear yourself admit to yourself that you were wrong. You goofed. You made a mistake. Sometimes that admission will require an accompanying apology without which the admission of your fallibility will be hollow and ineffective. Sometimes your ownership of the admission will not be complete unless you share it with someone you trust – not to seek forgiveness (when necessary, get that from God, or from anyone harmed by your mistake) but only to get reassurance that you were, in fact, wrong, and are now dealing with the issue honestly.

How often have you heard the expression, 'an honest mistake'? Honest mistakes happen. Honest or dishonest, your mistakes can be forgiven and forgotten, and you can get on with your life ... if you have the will to do exactly that.

Perhaps this is easier said than done. But read on.

TWO IMAGES

Imagine a sign over the entrance to your workplace that reads: 'The person who never makes a mistake, hardly ever makes anything'. That translates to the comforting assurance that there is a place in this world, including the world of work, for you and your mistakes.

Or, if you are handcuffed psychologically to past mistakes – if, in other words, you carry them like luggage wherever you go – find a psychological equivalent of those roller suitcases you see in airports and *let your past mistakes stop weighing you down.*

You may need professional help – pastoral or psychological – to get your release from this kind of burden. If you need help, seek it out. One solid and sobering principle of spirituality instructs that 'grace builds on nature'. You can ignore neither the laws of nature nor the remedies available to you on the natural level, if you want to keep both yourself and your career on track.

VALUES

A writer friend of mine, whom I first met when he was well into middle age, surprised me with the disclosure that his present wife was not his first. 'I made a mistake the first time', he said. 'I married my first wife for her looks; I married my present wife for her values.'

Forget for the moment that his (quite attractive) second wife might not be completely charmed by the comparison, and that my opposition to divorce would prompt me to want to probe the possibility of living with some of one's mistakes. Think instead of the role of values in mistake *prevention*.

An internalised centre for mistake control could provide effective answers from within by bringing your deeply held values to the surface in the face of important decisions. The nine Pauline principles come to mind in this regard. When you let your values decide, you are less likely to make mistakes. This, of course, presumes that you have the proper values – that what you cherish, consider worth your time and effort, and would refuse to trade or trifle away, is thoroughly good.

Your values cannot rise to the surface if you have not first permitted them to be planted in your soul. That 'planting' is the work of spirituality. Nor will they rise spontaneously unless you have lifted them up in reflective awareness often, even daily, in the style of the morning and evening exercises outlined for you in Chapter 1.

Think of love, joy, peace, patience, kindness, generosity, faithfulness, gentleness and self-control as values. Use them as rangefinders when you look at upcoming decisions. Frame your choices within these values; if the fit is bad, or just uncomfortable, think some more before you choose. You'll never know how many mistakes that reflective pause will enable you to avoid.

In Thomas Heywood's 1607 play, *A Woman Killed with Kindness*, you will find these lines – part prayer, part exasperation. These words deserve a place in any spirituality intended to help you live with your mistakes:

O God, O God, that it were possible
To undo things done, to call back yesterday,
That Time could turn up his swift sandy glass,
To untell the days, and to redeem the hours.

The upturned hourglass cannot, alas, bring back time already spent, where your mistakes are buried. It can, however, measure the present as it makes its way into the future, where your mistakes can be overcome.

PART THREE

SPIRITUAL PILLARS FOR THE WORLD OF WORK

CHAPTER FOURTEEN
SECOND STARTS

I once heard an ever-so-earnest executive make the following pronouncement, spoken, of course, over a stiff upper lip: 'Yesterday we stood on the brink of disaster, and today we took a great step forward!' Anyone who has made it this far in this book may now recall one or two personal experiences with the 'brink of disaster' in a cursory review of his or her own past reversals.

It would be a healthy exercise if such a review were accompanied by a sober anticipation of future setbacks. But any review, retrospective or prospective, should be made in light of a well-thought-out strategy for recovery. You certainly don't want your resolute 'step forward' to take you over the cliff!

PREVENTION AND RECOVERY

It is time now to reflect on a positive strategy of prevention and recovery – relative to all the reversals outlined in this book – that is reinforced by a faith-based spirituality. Rebound strategies are yours to plan.

The objective of this and the remaining chapters in this book is to encourage the conviction that you can rebound from virtually all the reversals you meet in the workplace or other circumstances of life. It is largely up to you. The Pauline Criteria, sketched out for you in 'scorecard' form for your daily use in Chapter 1, can, if assimilated, propel you along the strategic path these final few chapters will outline for you.

Let me emphasise: these steps are yours to take on the road to recovery from any, and I mean any, reversal. You can learn wisdom by just observing what happened to you in those unguarded moments when you were not wise. The consequences of your foolishness may last a lifetime, but you are always free (and always able) to start again.

STARTING OVER

Christianity is a religion of second starts. Anyone who tries to push nature too far – attempting, for example, to defy the law of gravity – will discover how unforgiving nature can be. But anyone imbued with the principles of Christian spirituality will be convinced of the availability at any time, of mercy, and the readiness of God to grant forgiveness whenever you ask for it honestly. That's the disposition you need to set yourself up for a fresh start.

The early morning and late evening reflection exercise recommended for your consideration and outlined in Chapter 1 is an invitation to begin again every day. But understand: this is not a forget-what's-behind-and-be-prepared-for-anything-that-comes approach; this is a strategic new beginning in light of past mistakes. It is strategic in the sense of being grounded in a sense of purpose (your personal mission statement), a purpose that provides you with a clear sense of direction. It is strategic also in the sense of laying out a step-by-step recovery plan.

How do you begin your new beginning? Consider whether or not forgiveness (of yourself or of others who may have injured you) should be the first step in your recovery strategy from a workplace reversal. If you refuse to forgive yourself for past mistakes, large or small, you will never get off to a fresh start. If you refuse to forgive others, your feet may well be encased in the cement of hatred. Chapter 16 will help you reflect on the importance of forgiveness.

No, you cannot undo the past. Yes, it is impossible to upend the hourglass of events and run them through again. But there is a future that is beginning now, and a new stream of events can start at any time you are willing to let them begin.

Second starts (which, over time, can be multiplied as long as life lasts) always look to the future. If initiated under the impulse of a faith-based spirituality, these new beginnings do not represent a fuzzy faith in the future; they represent a faith in God who *owns* the future and who holds the human planner's destiny in his hands.

IDENTIFYING PROBLEMS

The success of any second start will depend on the accuracy of your identification of the issue that prompted the necessity of a rebound or recovery. In other words, you have to frame the issue correctly.

Take, for example, the case of a small subsidiary of a large corporation that I heard about recently. A management team of four or five peers, all talented people in their late thirties and early forties, was functioning well under the informal leadership of a woman regarded as 'first among equals'. She was, for all practical purposes, head of the subsidiary as she also served on the board of the parent corporation. Suddenly, one of her peers was elevated – that is to say, formally appointed – to head the subsidiary.

Stress fuelled by anger, resentment, jealousy, and hurt feelings set in. Management group harmony and productivity in the subsidiary suffered, until outside intervention in the form of professional consultants helped those adversely affected by the decision to 'reframe' the issue and identify it for what it truly was. This was not an issue of ambition on the part of another or unfair advantage taken by another; it turned out to be an issue of personal loss. Once a formal leader was named, the members of the management team each had to come to terms with the fact that he or she had not been selected to lead the subsidiary.

The others came to recognise their discontent for what it was: the experience of loss, a loss of their respective dreams or fantasies of personal achievement. Their hopes had been dashed. The recovery strategy had to begin with a focus on human hope in each member (and in the team as a whole). Reframing in this way – discovering the real issue rather than being distracted by buzzwords or technicalities – is a good way to gain insight and clarity in identifying an appropriate first step in a second start.

TALKING AND LISTENING

Successful second starts often require having someone to talk to before setting out on a new course. If you talk and the right person listens, stress can be released and clarity achieved.

Here is a description, written in his own words in a letter to me, of how a faith-committed entrepreneur, who is a successful CEO in the recycling industry, worked through a stressful situation in making a good second start for a troubled company.

> When I took over as CEO of my company, it was in serious trouble. Gross revenues had fallen by one-third; we were losing serious money (in the hundreds of thousands of dollars), and backlog (signed contracts for future business) was barely one year's sales rather than the more than two years we consider comfortable.
>
> I began to feel the stress almost immediately. In the early days after I took over, we had to lay off staff that had been with us for a long time, stretch out payments wherever we could, renegotiate our bank loan. In the first few months, things got worse before they got better and I suspect some staff had doubts whether we would survive.
>
> Of the many ways I tried to reduce the stress, four worked. For some years, I had a routine of praying and meditating at 5:30 each morning. To this I added journaling three or four times a week. I also was much more conscientious about seeing my spiritual director. The prospect of such meetings kept me from abandoning journaling at times when it seemed stale or when I encountered lots of internal resistance, or apathy, or whatever. She also provided me with someone besides my wife to whom I could pour out my frustration, fears, resentments, etc. Lastly, I was very fortunate to have a protégé (now CEO) in whom I knew I could confide and who shared my conviction that we could turn things around.
>
> I do not know which of these was more important, but I do believe that I might not have pulled it off had I not

had another male, in this case someone from within the company, in whom I could confide with total candour. I say this because in my experience most men in the business world have good friends but not really confidants in the same way that, judging from my wife, women do. Men seem much more reluctant totally to let go of their 'successful businessman' masks or whatever masks they are wearing.

We were able to bring in new business within a few months, and fortunately we kept the confidence and trust of our clients and Board throughout. But it took close to two years before we could climb back to profitability and even longer to convince our bankers and others that things really had turned around for good.

WILL IS NOT ENOUGH

Reframing the issue was necessary in the case of the disillusioned management group dealing with the elevation of a peer; there the second-start strategy began with a re-examination of the subject of personal hope. A four-point strategy of prayer, keeping a journal, seeking spiritual counselling, and talking things out with a business confidant worked well in the case of the CEO who faced a serious decline in his company's performance.

A solid second start requires more than just the will to begin again. It takes faith in yourself and in your ability (with the help of friends) to get back on your feet, cranked up, and moving forward.

The unbeliever may say that is all it takes. But the believer knows it also takes faith in God, the God with whom you connect through a functioning spirituality, the God who holds your destiny in all-powerful, all-loving hands that are reaching out towards you at every moment of your existence, in good times and in bad. And more often than not, simply because this is the way God wills to work, it takes a human intermediary through whom God chooses to work in order to touch you right there where you are – in your personal corner of the human predicament.

This point is worth considering closely. You will not be touched unless you reach out for help, unless you take that first step and give another human being a chance to help you.

ASKING FOR HELP

Why is it that most of us find it so hard to ask for help? The first (and almost always accurate) answer to that question is simple: pride.

Pride is a tricky trait. It is to some degree necessary for the proper maintenance of self-esteem. But pride can get out of hand very easily. When it does, it sometimes moves in very deceptive ways. Open yourself up here to a moment of honest reflection.

You normally think of pride in others in association with power, even arrogance, and you expect pride to manifest itself in bluster and aggressive action. But pride often borrows humility's garb and becomes harder to identify.

When pride withdraws from the front rank it does so as a protective measure. What is being protected is, of course, one's proud estimate of one's own superiority and independence. Perhaps you know from personal experience that unless you are willing to 'come off it', acknowledge that you have two flat feet of clay, and ask for help, your second start could be deferred indefinitely, possibly forever.

If spirituality has anything at all to teach you, the lesson learned will be that you are not independent. Acting as if you are completely independent is an exercise in practical atheism; it gives the lie to whatever pious proclamations you may make on Sunday when you go to church.

The remarkably practical Book of Proverbs can serve up a working principle to guide your reflection at just about any step in a strategic second start: 'Pride goes before disaster, and a haughty spirit before a fall' (16:18). This is the familiar verse that you often hear collapsed into the dictum, 'pride goeth before the fall'. Heed that 'haughty spirit' warning always. And rest your second start on the solid spiritual foundation offered in an earlier verse of Proverbs: 'Entrust your works to the Lord, and your plans will succeed' (16:3).

CHAPTER FIFTEEN
FAITH AT WORK

Faith at work within you is one thing; faith in you at work is something else again. There can be a gap between practising one's religious faith (being an 'observant Jew', a 'practising Catholic') and living it. What does it mean to practise your religion, if you don't live it every day? Having it, so to speak, but not living it, would seem to reduce faith to some kind of label for social identification, instead of making faith the content of a committed life.

The split between the faith that good people profess before God and the horizonless lives they live in their respective workplaces is surely a contributor to the joyless approach so many people in the workforce take to their jobs. Anyone who succeeds in closing that gap can begin to better understand what the balanced believer I quoted earlier – a man who is well aware of the importance of having a day-in, day-out sense of vocation – meant when he remarked, 'If you really feel called to what you do, you'll never work a day in your life!'

NO TIME-OUTS

If you are a believer, a person whose faith commitment is real, and free, and rooted in God, something of great spiritual significance is going on within you all the time.

Faith works wonders within you in all situations. It gifts you now with a share in God's own life and love that you would not otherwise have. It promises you eternal security, salvation that you could never under any circumstances gain on your own. 'We carry this treasure', writes St Paul, speaking of grace, 'in earthen vessels' (2 Cor 4:7). Earthen vessels can drop and break.

We are free to reject God's gifts; we are thus always at risk of dropping the vessel and losing both faith and grace. Far too many believers live with a dualistic mindset that separates 'otherworldly' considerations, like faith and grace, from this world's workplace realities of give and take, of getting and spending in the human community.

There is an African proverb that says, 'This world is a marketplace; the other world is home'. But even the marketplace can be a place of grace. The whole purpose of the practical workplace spirituality presented in this book is to help you close that dualistic gap and bridge the this-world–other-world attitudinal divide.

A healthy spirituality will not encourage you to 'hate' or flee the world; it will not reward any attempt to 'bury' your treasure for safekeeping. It will encourage your engagement with the world of work for the service of others and the glory of God, who created it all and wants your help in developing the gift of creation to the fullest. Only a balanced person need apply for this kind of work.

BALANCE AND THE PAULINE VALUES

Balance begins with an awareness that faith is, in fact, at work within you and that you are, therefore, alive in the Spirit. This will set you apart as one who is in balance, on target, and at peace. The less apart you find yourself to be, or, to put it in positive terms, the more you find yourself to be just one among many who are balanced, on target, and at peace with themselves in their transit through life, so much the better the workaday world will be!

Faith in you at work represents transformative potential for the workplace. There is no room for pulpits or pamphlets, sermons or proselytising in your place of employment (unless you work for a church, synagogue, shrine, or mosque!). Such activity would be altogether inappropriate, unfair and unwise. The transformation that faith can bring to office, factory, store, laboratory, construction site, transportation systems, or any other place where daily bread is earned (including church-related employment), is in the form of human love, joy, peace, patience, kindness, generosity, faithfulness, gentleness and self-control.

If you think yourself incapable of bringing these nine Pauline values to birth in the workplace, you are not giving your own human potential a fair reading. If you recognise your capability, but say something to the effect that, although your spirit is willing your flesh (that is, your capacity to activate these values) is weak, I would argue that you are not giving faith and grace a fair chance to get to work within you. I'd suggest that you spend some time with the morning-and-evening checklist outlined in Chapter 1 and prayerfully consider the relevance of the nine Pauline Criteria in your life.

ENTRUSTING YOURSELF

Faith is the act by which you entrust yourself to God. It is not, however, purely volitional; it is a matter of both will and intellect.

I have a friend whose single favourite Shakespeare line of all time is King Henry's response to a report that the French are poised for battle against him at Agincourt, and ready to charge. Having just made his soul-stirring, confidence-building Saint Crispin's Day speech to his outnumbered soldiers, Henry responds to the news of imminent attack by saying: 'All things are ready, if our minds be so' (*The Life of King Henry the Fifth*, Act IV, Scene iii). And the Earl of Westmoreland comments: 'Perish the man whose mind is backward now!'

ALL THINGS ARE READY, IF YOUR MIND IS READY

Henry seems to rejoice in the overwhelming odds (five to one against him) in the face of a powerful enemy. Logic says flee; faith (assuming, of course, that your cause is just) says trust, and give full credit to God for the victory that faith assures you is on its way. Practical faith means having your *mind* in the right place.

You should know your faith. That means putting yourself in touch with the sources of God's revelation to you: scripture (which you probably have on a bookshelf at home) and tradition (a term that refers to the understanding of God's revelation that the church has been 'handing down' generation to generation in doctrine, practice, sermons, ritual, and memory).

Make the effort, take the time to put yourself in touch with scripture and tradition. The relationship of the word 'tradition' to the verb 'trade' is worth exploring here. The Latin verb 'tradere' means to 'hand over'. Trade moves items from one hand to another; tradition literally hands down, generation to generation, something considered worth preserving in the lives of like-minded people.

In the words of the Second Vatican Council, 'Sacred Scripture is the speech of God as it is put down in writing under the breath of the Holy Spirit' (*Dei Verbum*, n. 9). If you are a believer, such a characterisation should remind you that you can listen to that 'speech of God' simply by taking the Bible off the shelf and setting some time aside for reflective reading. And although you don't have to set up camp within a church structure or surround yourself with scholarly books to get in touch with tradition, it would seem prudent and wise to put yourself closer to this second source of revelation both through some exposure to history, theology and social teaching, and through participation in liturgical worship.

If you find yourself wincing now at the thought of these 'formal' observances, or saying, 'Not for me', you may want to ask yourself: how you are going to feed the faith-based spirituality that you need to sustain yourself in the workplace?

'CAMPAIGN HEADQUARTERS'

I know a man of considerable depth in both faith and wealth who exercises responsible stewardship, is eminently practical, and devoutly religious. He once told me that he thinks of the place of worship called 'church' as a 'campaign headquarters'. 'You go there for inspiration, nourishment, and strategy,' he said, 'but you go there in order to go out again, not to devote time, talent and treasure to building a *bigger* campaign headquarters.' You go there, in other words, so that you can be sufficiently energised to put your faith to work. And you should leave there to return to work on Monday morning with a prayer like this in your heart:

Lord, God, work is your gift to us,
a call to reach new heights by using our talents for
    the good of all.
Guide us as we work and teach us to live
    in the spirit that has made us your sons and daughters,
in the love that has made us brothers and sisters.
('Daytime Prayer for Midmorning on Monday', *Christian Prayer: The Liturgy of the Hours*, New York: Catholic Book Publishing Co., 1976, pp. 1001–1002).

If love is a reality not normally associated with your return to work on Monday morning, perhaps you should consider closely the next chapter, whose topic is forgiveness. It is possible that your inability to accept yourself as a loved sinner, one who is both forgiven and loved, may be impeding your ability to forgive others and find them lovable. Or, you may just consider it impractical, even silly, to make a place for love ('the love that has made us brothers and sisters') in the workplace.

The same St Paul who passed along the nine wisdom principles you've been pondering on your way through these pages, had a very practical, down-to-earth explanation of the meaning of love. He spelled it out in the thirteenth chapter of his First Letter to the Corinthians:

Love is always patient and kind; it is never jealous; love is never boastful or conceited; it is never rude or selfish; it does not take offence, and is not resentful.
Love takes no pleasure in other people's sins but delights in the truth; it is always ready to excuse, to trust, to hope, and to endure whatever comes.
Love does not come to an end.

The late Rabbi Abraham Joshua Heschel had the workplace in mind when he said, 'Our concern is not how to worship in the catacombs, but how to remain human in the skyscrapers'. Faith at work can humanise the workplace; it can also guarantee a place for love in the most secular nine-to-five surroundings.

CHAPTER SIXTEEN
FORGIVENESS

The healing power of forgiveness cannot be overemphasised. Whether given or received, forgiveness heals. And regardless of whether it comes to you from God or another human being, forgiveness is a matchless gift.

REFUSING TO FORGIVE
In a book entitled, *Hearts That We Broke Long Ago* (Bantam, 1983), the Canadian writer Merle Shain wrote:

> Until one forgives, life is governed by an endless cycle of resentments and retaliations, and we spend our days scratching at the scabs of the wounds that we sustained long ago instead of letting them dry up and disappear. There is no way to hate another that does not cost the hater, no way to remain unforgiving without maiming yourself, because undissolved anger stutters through the body of the person who cannot forgive.

That 'undissolved anger' can be the source of deep depression. If you feel depressed right now, it is possible that you are, in Shain's words, 'maiming yourself' by your refusal to forgive others. You may also be refusing to forgive yourself and thus permitting yourself to be your own worst enemy.

Here again, it is appropriate to note the importance of talking things over with others whom you respect and trust. Like any other mortal, you are not the best judge in your own case. In opening up to others who have no ax to grind, you may discover your persistent (and perhaps initially unconscious) refusal to forgive yourself. If the persons in whom you confide are true friends, and if you give them the opportunity to do so, they can help you come to realise that you are acting destructively towards others and even towards yourself.

Jim Wallis, the pastor of Sojourners Community in Washington, DC, and longtime editor of *Sojourners* magazine, says, 'The idea of forgiveness often seems abstract and "religious" in an otherworldly kind of way. But in fact forgiveness is very practical and necessary for human life on the planet to survive ... When we refuse to forgive, the cycle of vengeance, retaliation, and violence just escalates ... It's only genuine forgiveness that breaks the cycle of destruction and opens up new possibilities.'

RECONCILIATION

The Sermon on the Mount, which contains some firm instruction against retaliation, addressed the issue of forgiveness in the context of worship. Your refusal to forgive would make you unworthy to stand before the altar. 'If you bring your gift to the altar and there recall that your brother or sister has anything against you, leave your gift at the altar, go first to be reconciled with your brother or sister, and then come and offer your gift' (Matthew 5:23-24).

I believe that one of the best ways to face up to your responsibility to forgive another is to offer a gift to that person. There is no parallel, of course, between your gift to God, as referenced in the saying of Jesus above, and any gift you might offer to someone who has injured you. All the same, Jesus' radical teaching on forgiveness could be taken as encouragement not only to leave your gift at the altar, but to put another gift, one that symbolises your forgiveness, into the hand of the one who hurt you.

A practical spirituality will surely have you measure your performance against the standard embodied in the Lord's Prayer: 'Forgive us our trespasses, as we forgive those who trespass against us'. Realise that, in making this prayer, you are asking to be forgiven on a contingent basis. You are declaring yourself to be willing to be forgiven only if you forgive others. This is a remarkable standard. No one is perfect, of course, but no one can dodge that standard; it will be there to challenge you every day of your life. The stakes are always high; the choice is always yours.

OPENING UP

A great humanist, Maynard Mack, once remarked that if you could reduce everything Shakespeare ever wrote to one word, that word would be 'forgiveness'. I don't know enough about Shakespeare's works to comment on that, except to say that anyone who understands human nature as well as Shakespeare did will certainly have a respect for the power of forgiveness in helping you find your way through the human predicament.

Add to all this the bonus promised in an ancient spiritual maxim: 'If you do not close your ear to others, you open God's ear to yourself'. When someone seeks your forgiveness; you are being given an opportunity. Pay attention and respond appropriately; realise, too, that you are giving others the chance to grow in grace whenever you ask forgiveness of them.

THE NEED TO FORGIVE

Here is an example where an unmet need to forgive all but crippled a promising career.

Not long ago, there was a rising star in a large insurance company who was sent by his employer to a distant city to reinvigorate a troubled branch of the organisation. Described as a 'charger with a great analytical mind', this man was nevertheless losing some of his 'charge' in this new assignment. He found himself unable to think things through as easily and clearly as he had done before. He found the situation to be a lot worse than he had been led to believe.

The worse it looked to him, the more distressed he got. Heavy layoffs were necessary; workplace morale plummeted. In the face of these challenges, the 'superstar' manager became volatile and showed evidence of increasing disorganisation.

Were these heavy workplace demands *all* that were troubling him? The answer, it turned out, was 'no'. In consultation with John Fontana and David Deacon of Morrison Associates, he disclosed that his wife was ill and incapacitated; there was no support from his relocated family as he tried to meet his mounting and more challenging workplace demands. He also was operating without the support of his church. In his youth, he was educated at an Episcopal boarding school where he was helped a lot by a clergyman whom he admired. He even considered a career in ministry at that time. Before taking on his new assignment, this manager had long been active in the church. When he presented himself at a church in his new location, he was asked 'to send his references' from the former pastor; this soured him on the new congregation and he never went back.

Even so, the consulting psychologist, David Deacon, told him, 'I think the issue in your not going to church is your anger with God'. Together, the manager and the psychologist focused on the issue of anger. They noticed that although his boss thought relations between them were smooth, things were not all that smooth on the side of this manager who thought he had been misled into thinking it was really a 'little fix', not a 'monster turnaround' that was called for when he was transferred. He was in fact angry: with the boss for less than full disclosure; with his wife for being ill and non-supportive; with God for letting it all happen.

But he was afraid to admit to being angry with God. The way out for him, according to David Deacon, was forgiveness. 'He had to forgive himself for getting angry with God and for being so grandiose that he thought he could judge God', said Deacon. 'He also had to forgive God for "doing" whatever it was that he thought God had done to him; and he had to forgive his boss for putting him out on a limb, and his wife for getting sick.'

'Grace is necessary for forgiveness; there is no way you can earn grace.' These insightful words from David Deacon underscore the need for a functioning spirituality on the rebound and recovery route.

In commenting on his role in this case, John Fontana noted that another issue here was this man's need for structures. He went into a new environment without familiar structures or old friends. Social support previously received from church connections vanished. Family support was withheld and, once he was in the distant city, there was noticeably less support from the company. Before the change, when support structures were in place, he had become 'overly self-reliant', said Fontana, 'and he didn't have to use power and authority'. In the new setting where he needed cooperation and support, he fell back on a power-and-authority device, namely, volatile behaviour. Disruptions cause stress, commented Fontana, 'The more you ask people to change, the more affect is an issue'. In other words, *feelings* surface with the stress; you have to watch that the horse does not throw the rider.

Once he assimilated all this 'feedback' from the consultation, the manager settled down and turned the operation and himself around. He extended a measure of forgiveness to himself so that he could learn from this experience and move ahead. In time, he returned the branch to profitability and regained control of his life.

NO WAY TO HATE WITHOUT DIMINISHING

It would be difficult to exaggerate the power of forgiveness at home or on the job. It takes a large-hearted person to decide to forgive; by the act of forgiving the heart of the forgiver becomes even larger.

Forgiveness fastens friendships; anyone interested in contributing to the return of loyalty to the workplace might simply look for opportunities to forgive. And anyone who can count should take a moment to calculate in measurable, practical workplace terms the value of the lesson that is available to all in the words of Merle Shain: 'There is no way to hate another that does not cost the hater, no way to remain unforgiving without maiming yourself.'

Try to build forgiveness into your life. This is a project with two dimensions and countless manifestations.

The upward dimension, so to speak, is your need to seek God's forgiveness for yourself. Nobody is perfect. You know that, but how deeply within your heart can you locate that knowledge?

Acting as if you stand in no need at all of forgiveness is blind arrogance. Factor a simple request for forgiveness into your evening review of the day just ended. You are in God's presence. You will notice that there have been failures during the day. Acknowledge them and ask your Creator to make you whole.

The other dimension of forgiveness in your life is outward: out to those who have ignored you, offended you, injured you. This dimension will have innumerable manifestations. Do all that is in your power to make those broken relationships whole. At least you can build the bridge from your side as far out as you can, hoping in the best of faith for a connection from the other side.

All you can do is try. And you have to try, or else you give the lie to a spirituality rooted in love, peace and generosity. Your effort requires you to do more than simply keep the door open; it is clearly not enough simply 'to live and let live'.

Genuine creativity involves making something out of nothing. From the 'nothing' of your evacuated pride – from your humility – your forgiveness can create strong new relationships. And here, again, you will never know unless you try!

You are familiar with Alexander Pope's dictum: 'To err is human, to forgive, divine'. You have often heard that it is wise to 'forgive and forget', although Shakespeare put that proposition the other way round on the lips of King Lear: 'Pray you now, forget and forgive'. You will never be divine, but you can imitate divinity in forgiving. You may never be able to forget, but you can act as if you have whenever you forgive from the heart. In either case, true forgiveness is the restorative measure, the transforming decision that puts you on a brand new page.

> Turn away your face from my sins;
>   blot out all my guilt.
> A clean heart create for me, God;
>   renew in me a steadfast spirit. (Psalm 51:11-12)

CHAPTER SEVENTEEN
VERACITY

Truth telling is a healthy, wonderfully restorative character trait that carries with it significant practical benefits. Anyone who makes a regular habit of telling the truth will find life simpler and considerably less complicated than a person who lies as a matter of course.

The lives of those who always have to remember how they altered or distorted the facts in past statements, or how they spun out stories totally unrelated to the truth are anything but worry free. As a general rule, their own duplicity divides their hearts. Their memories as well as their morals are strained. And people notice. (You may have known someone for whom the old joke was applicable: 'He doesn't murder the truth, he doesn't even get close enough to do it bodily harm.')

From your own experience, you would probably agree that people who exhibit calm, enjoy peace of heart, and know what it means to lead a balanced life are, as a general rule, people who can be relied upon to tell the truth. This is not the philosophy portrayed in the old cartoon that pictures a harried secretary standing by the desk of a boss who lectures her as follows: 'Yes, Miss Jones, honesty *is* the best policy, but it just isn't *company* policy'.

FREEDOM

Over the entrance to the Lauinger Library on the campus of Georgetown University, these famous words from the Gospel of John are inscribed: 'You will know the truth and the truth will set you free' (8:32). That's why students (and others) use libraries: to search out the truth and gain their freedom from ignorance.

Truth is liberating. In a theological sense, it frees you from sin. In a practical, day-to-day, workplace sense, the truth teller is a free person, recognised as a person of integrity who has not simply something to say, but a self to commit, a self that is out there, on the line, with any statement he or she makes.

Instinctively, you dismiss the prevaricator, the perjurer, the liar, as unreliable, not to be trusted, as being shallow in a fundamental way. You trust the truth teller as a person of significant depth and genuine character. You know there is something there, deep within.

Thomas Wolfe, writing with an anti-capitalist bias in his 1934 novel *You Can't Go Home Again*, let his own prejudices show through in his protagonist's description of that 'type look' he had come to recognise 'as belonging to the race of small business men':

> It was a look which he had discovered to be common to all members of this race whether they lived in Holland, England, Germany, France, the United States, Sweden, or Japan. There was a hardness and grasping quality in it that showed in the prognathous jaw. There was something a little sly and tricky about the eyes, something a little amoral in the sleekness of the flesh, something about the dry concavity of the face and its vacuous expression in repose which indicated a grasping self-interest and a limited intellectual life.

My own intellectual life was one notch less limited after I consulted a dictionary to discover the meaning of 'prognathous'. (It means 'having jaws that protrude'.) This unflattering portrayal of a sadly familiar business 'type' might encourage some men and women in business to take steps to ensure that the caricature will never be applicable to them.

What is the point of inserting this quotation from Thomas Wolfe's depressing (and Depression-Conditioned) characterisation here? I mean to use it to highlight an element of truth about the absence of truthfulness. I think it is fair to say that 'grasping self-interest' is usually all that is needed to explain the motive that is operative when the truth is bent or broken in the workplace.

Take the opposite tack to set the direction of your personal style. Use nothing 'sly or tricky' in your approach to others; exercise your own tight control over the 'hardness and grasping quality' that the business culture can encourage, and thus adopt for yourself a 'countercultural' attitude over and against the excesses of the business culture.

SELF-CONTROL AND THE HONEST SELF

The ninth of the Pauline Criteria – self-control – has as much relevance to the way you conduct yourself in the office as it does to your behaviour at the bar or dinner table. Success, in the sense of balance and contentment, in the workplace depends in no small measure on your ability to tell the truth (at least to yourself) about yourself. And that certainly requires a measure of disciplined self-control.

David Morrison tells an interesting story about a thirty-five-year-old female business executive whose effectiveness was hindered by her inability to expose her vulnerability – to ask for help. She was painfully shy and she had trouble admitting her shyness even to herself.

In high school, this very bright, energetic and attractive person had decided to adapt to her shyness as she searched out a place for herself in the adolescent social scene. She adopted what Morrison calls a 'masculine' achievement strategy. She did not realise, however, that the boys were shy. The more she achieved, the more she removed herself from the boys she hoped to attract. She was unaware, says Morrison, that her presence, her apparent poise and self-assurance made the adolescent boys feel vulnerable and uncomfortable. At age thirty-five she was still doing this. The 'script' she worked out of in business was tilted towards achievement instead of attachment (that is, cooperative participation with a team). She didn't understand that in order to get the productive business relationships she wanted (as well as a meaningful personal relationship), she had to expose her vulnerability. She needed to acknowledge exactly where she was, accept her vulnerability, and ask for help. This truth would set her free for success in business – and, indeed, in other areas of life.

CANDOUR

Another issue in the matter of truth-telling in the workplace (as well as in interpersonal relationships) might best be categorised under the heading of 'candour', which should never be confused with rudeness or aggressiveness for the sake of being aggressive. You will hear different opinions expressed concerning the value of bluntness in on-the-job discussions that are expected to produce decisions. Some appreciate it; others resent it. If a person who wants, for the good of the decision-making process, to be candid – making sure that all the facts, pleasant and unpleasant, are on the table – he or she runs the risk of having candour mistaken for rudeness, blunt arrogance, or an opinionated attempt to dominate the conversation. If you are convinced that candour is important – something that you should bring to the table – it is your duty to do so diplomatically.

You should welcome, even invite, assistance from the person chairing the discussion in the form of that person's asking the others at the table, 'How does that strike you? Do you agree with that?' This opens the door to immediate clarification or qualification from others on what's been said, thus encouraging your candour and not letting social pressure muzzle your desire to speak the truth.

It is good leadership if the person chairing the meeting gets *all* the 'pros' and 'cons' on the table and urges all participants in the decision-making process to speak to *both* sides of the question before it is resolved. This requires freedom; perhaps this is the freedom associated with veracity in the scriptural dictum, 'the truth will set you free'. To point to the 'something good' that you know to be present in an option you do not favour could diminish the chances of 'winning' the argument for the option you prefer. The question, however, is: do you prefer that option for the right reasons – is it 'right' from the perspective of the greater good of the whole organisation?

It is also very good leadership if the manager of the meeting can get participants to disclose how they feel about both sides of the issue. Seeing something good on both sides of a question is not insincerity or make-believe; any question important enough to be 'on the table' and under review for eventual resolution certainly has two sides. But honesty – the search for truth – requires a willingness to determine *why you feel* one way or another about a proposed option, and it requires that you express your ease or unease about accepting a given possible outcome.

Your feelings can function as windows on your motives, and your motives may, as you well know, be elevated or base, narrowly self-interested or rooted in the common good. Veracity implies vulnerability, a willingness to be open to full disclosure of the true origin of the answer emerging at this moment from within.

This is not just tricky terrain that I have you walking through at the moment (it is always difficult to understand one's true motives); it is also sacred ground. You are much more than the sum of your feelings, of course, but it is helpful to recognise that your feelings connect you to the presence or the absence of the Spirit within. The feeling alone, the affect, is not enough to provide an answer. You have to know *why* you feel as you do in the face of a decision to be made. A feeling of fear, for example, could be there because you understand your limits in facing up to a challenge the Spirit would have you meet; it could also be there because you know the decision will involve the loss of something you possess and want to retain for purely selfish reasons (thus influencing you to resist the call the Spirit wants you to heed).

All that would apply to candour in workplace meetings applies as well to candour in those 'meetings' that take place between your ears when you are alone and trying to decide. You are a complicated person, precisely because you are a person (not because you happen to be you). Personhood is complicated. So is life. You, as a person, cannot make it through life without dealing with the complications. And your gyroscope on this journey is your veracity.

SEEKING THE TRUTH

Being a truth-seeker, a truth-teller, a truth-lover is your assurance that you are in balance and on target as you move from one moment to the next in a journey of unknown duration, through intermediate goals you cannot always clearly identify, towards an eternal goal of security in the God of all truthfulness, who can be seen by you now only through the eyes of faith.

Spirituality has a wonderful potential for keeping you on course. It also keeps you grounded in humility, which is the special soil of sacred ground. From the depths of your humility, you will find veracity and you will see the truth. And you will, if you are like me, add an 'Amen' to this poetic wisdom from George Herbert: 'Dare to be true: nothing can need a lie;/A fault, which needs it most, grows two thereby.' Consider, too, these words from the psalter:

> Good and upright is the Lord,
>   who shows sinners the way,
> Guides the humble rightly,
>   and teaches the humble the way ...
> Who are those who fear the Lord?
>   God shows them the way to choose.
> They live well and prosper ... (Psalm 25:8-9, 12-13)

CHAPTER EIGHTEEN
CREATIVITY

Creativity is a form of generativity. Who has ever experienced the thrill of becoming a parent and not known something akin to the psychological surge that can be produced by rebound and recovery from past setbacks? It is all there: the freshness of a new beginning, the expectant hope, the conviction that something all-powerful is at work in this 'blessed event'. You just know that an abundance of good things is on its way. You are upbeat; you are smiling. The setbacks, like labour pains, are all behind you.

Recovery through creativity is a wonderful way to rebound from reversals in or out of the workplace. Creativity engages both mind and heart; it requires sensitivity. Whatever metaphor you choose to use in describing it, your engines are running, your juices are flowing, your eye is on the future. Creativity is your best weapon against the limitations that try to hem you in. Creativity enables you to 'run away' without ever leaving home.

HOW TO DO IT

Now, of course, no one can command you to 'be creative'. You cannot just make up your mind that you are going to 'be creative'. You have to work, and work hard, at 'being creative'.

How? Imitation is one route, quite literally a 'free' way, open to all. Study the creative achievements of others. Read as much as you can; find out about the accomplishments and exploits that are chronicled in the history books or reported in the newspapers. Be alert to unusual ways of doing things; take note of the original and unconventional in what unobservant others might regard as ordinary surroundings. Learn how inventions and innovations first came to see the light of day.

Read biographies of creative people. Try to figure out how things work.

Some lights will go on in your mind; no need to apologise for enjoying the fruits of 'derivative' thinking. In the face of something new and interesting – an idea, a product or service, a slogan, a process – ask yourself: why didn't I think of that ... And what could I think of now that is just as impressive? Then wait for an answer!

This is not by way of preamble to your new career as inventor-entrepreneur, or writer-producer, or composer-director. You don't have to change your occupation or place of employment. The point is simply to re-engage yourself with your work in a creative way.

There are as-yet-undiscovered opportunities for you at work. There are new directions to explore in approaching old problems. There are potential collaborators out there whose creative potential you have not yet recognised. There may also be 'subordinates' just waiting for you to take US Army General George S. Patton's words to heart: 'Never tell people how to do things. Tell them what to do and they will surprise you with their ingenuity.'

Here's another thought to consider concerning creativity as it may unfold in the workplace: how many times have you nodded assent to the old saying that there is no limit to the good results you can produce, just so long as you are unconcerned about who gets the credit? And how often have you failed to act accordingly?

WORKING WITH OTHERS

Having spent all of my adult life in the academic workplace, I've noticed different approaches to work in different divisions or departments of the typical university. Some are intensely competitive: students trying to outpoint others for grades, for example, or faculty trying to outpace and outdistance colleagues on the research-and-publication track. I have also noticed others who are genuinely (and generously) cooperative. The competitors sometimes resort to forms of academic sabotage, while the collaborators freely share ideas and criticism. Architecture is one discipline where I have found both students and faculty to be characteristically collaborative; I will leave it to the reader to speculate on where competition typically gets out of control in other sections of the groves of academe. The point is that you can also apply the collaboration-competition framework to your own workplace setting. What aspects of your work lend themselves particularly well to cooperation?

Spirituality, as you have noticed in earlier sections of this book, recommends the integration of com-panionship (*cum-pane*) into workplace life. The collaborative cultivation of new ideas is just one manifestation of companionship.

I suspect that creativity and collaboration work well together. The opposite could be argued in the case of isolated writers and researchers who emerge after years of relative seclusion with genuinely creative results to show for their solitary labours. All the same, it seems reasonable to suggest that sensitive persons of open mind and generous heart can, working together in conscious collaboration, produce wonderfully creative outcomes, and, in the process, become closer friends. Hence the collaborative – not just the participative but the collaborative –workplace will, I would argue, be a happier, more productive place, a better place to work. Consciously taking this route back from your reversals will, I believe, help to put you clearly on a higher, better road.

COLLABORATION AND FEELING
Collaboration fosters outcomes that are more than the sum of the producing parts. And in the practice of collaboration, a bonding process develops that brings the collaborators closer together as friends. Collaborating friends in the workplace, who are in touch with their feelings (their affects) can change both the dynamic and the atmosphere of the organisation.

Creativity is always an exercise of intelligence. Before you conclude that only geniuses can be creative, recall that 'derivative' thinking can lead to creative outcomes. Even attempting to mimic the style or approach of another can lead you to positive, and distinctive, new initiatives.

The point to ponder here is that *thinking* – the exercise of intelligence – is within your power on or off the job. It is your birthright, yours to do at any time. In fact, it is your obligation to exercise your capacity to think, if you want to measure up to your full human potential. Thinking, then, is your task. Only remember that while the task is yours, the power is the Lord's.

Thinking is also immaterial. There is always enough for everyone. The more you think, the more – not less – there is for everyone else in the world of ideas. Creative thinking belongs in the realm of spirituality where the arithmetic is all addition and multiplication, where, as if by divine command, you and your ideas 'increase and multiply'.

EFFORT AND VISION
But none of this simply happens. Creativity demands your effort and, not infrequently, your cooperation with others. The effort will have you searching out the history of persons, ideas, innovations, successes and failures that explain how the place where you work, the product or service you produce, and the environment within which it all happens, got to be the way they are today. Your effort will have you looking out to *other* settings where other products and services are produced, and wondering what can be learned from that experience.

If, for example, you are employed in healthcare and are looking for creative ways to reduce errors and increase quality in patient care, a review of cockpit procedures for assuring airline passenger safety might prove unusually instructive. Your effort to make creative comparisons between the two areas is an exercise of intelligence. And whenever comparisons are being made, the opportunity for collaboration (with all due regard for avoiding anti-competitive activity) increases.

Creativity is indeed a spiritual pillar for you, as a believing person, in the world of work. Your belief looks ultimately towards an intelligent God, the God of all intelligence, the source of your intelligence. You believe that you are created in God's image and likeness, and although you cannot see God directly, you know *that you can know God in the effects of his creation.*

You can also know God from the sense you have of divine presence within you. There is probably a feeling dimension of your sense of that presence within you, but there is an even more enduring and pronounced intellectual dimension. By that I mean you may *feel* awkward and uncomfortable in saying that God talks to you, and you are properly skeptical of those who 'hear voices'. Faith, however, assures you that God communicates with you, works through you, cares for you, is present to you. This faith-knowledge should encourage and will certainly support your creative energies.

THE ALTERNATIVE

Not to be creative – simply choosing not to make any effort or participate in any collaborative search for new ways and new ideas – is to choose not to be spiritual. To let the senses alone decide your uses of time, your choices of right or wrong, better or worse, is to abdicate the higher side of your humanity. To leave your mind at home when you go to work, or your mind at work when you come back home, is to disengage yourself from the source of spiritual life and lead only half of your human life.

Creativity is an ignition key to spirituality. Turn it on and you ignite your mind. Your mind then engages with the countless other minds you find in print, in artistic imagination, in the voices of those around you. Creativity will ignite countless conversations, endless adventures in reading, and, if you let it happen, it will lead you, through a sense of wonder, to God.

It is not only regrettable, but tragic, that so many intelligent people live hemmed-in, self-centred lives, never really looking out or up, but only towards themselves. They failed along the way to gather up their share of enduring values for storage within their personhood. Once again, you have the problem of the empty centre. Preoccupation with weight loss and muscle tone accompanied by an enormous capacity for absorption of entertaining images, simply conditions self-enclosed people for passive spectatorship and consigns them to unfulfillment in a world where progress depends on creative contributions.

Where might you look for any of this in your set of Pauline Criteria? Try generosity (where the decision to make the effort resides), and don't forget that deep-down joy is part of every creative moment and the reward for every creative act. If these are part of creativity, it goes without saying that the Spirit is also there!

'In the beginning, when God created the heavens and the earth, the earth was a formless wasteland, and darkness covered the abyss ...' (Genesis 1:1) Ever since then, there has been a great deal of work to do. Human creativity participates in this work; it is an ongoing project. You are equipped to participate because God created man and woman in his image. Your creativity is rooted there; your creative roots run back to where it all began. In creativity, you can find the origin, the source, of your being.

CHAPTER NINETEEN
HELPING OTHERS

I like to think of service, or 'helping others', as turning your talents inside out. When you are on the rebound from serious personal or career reversals, it is a wise strategy to do things that help you get out of yourself. There's no better way to do this than to become intent on helping others. So many seemingly intractable problems – personal problems – will take care of themselves if you simply fix your attention on helping others. Once you become more concerned about easing the burdens of others than with having your own load lightened, you will, you may be sure, experience a new sense of freedom. You will also feel a whole lot better. Many people doubt that this principle will 'really work' for them, but that doubt dissolves after they've given this approach an honest try.

An old African proverb advises, 'God gives nothing to those who keep their arms crossed'. So open up your arms to others; reach out to others with a helping hand. And be prepared to receive more of the spiritual gifts God is always ready to share with you.

THE BENEFITS OF REACHING OUT
In work I've done over the years with job seekers (mid-career managers involuntarily separated from their jobs), I've noticed that those who had been involved as volunteers with outside organisations had a ready-made network of contacts to help them when they were out of work and looking. Those whose workaholic tendencies kept them tied up within their own places of employment found, when ousted, that their former workplace contacts were not so eager to assist.

With the rise of affluence in industrialised countries, there has been a proliferation of socially atomising appliances. You think it not at all unusual to have your private car, a single-family home, your personal phone (on your desk, in your car, and in your pocket), your computer (desktop, laptop, or hand-held), radio, and television set. You have ready access to a freezer, a microwave oven, and a host of other appliances. Your automatic washer and drier are ready when you are. You rarely have to borrow from or ask anyone for anything to meet your daily needs. Without a conscious choice on your part, you are now, for all practical purposes, sealed off from the human interaction previous generations enjoyed at the village well, the general store, the daily food market, the bus or train depot, and the public gathering places for recreation, worship, and communication. Not so very long ago, these points of contact were routine – even indispensable – parts of ordinary life. Now, in their absence or diminished presence, a commercially sanctioned culture of loneliness, isolation and alienation, has set in.

You have to deal with this first in yourself; the best way to do that is through service to others. You have daily opportunities to assist neighbours and others as they make their way through their similarly privatised, atomised lives. If only as a change of pace, why not shock someone by taking advantage of such an opportunity? Help carry up the groceries. Give up the taxi you just hailed. Bring in the mail. See what happens.

CONNECTIONS
Tom Mahon, a technology-marketing consultant in the San Francisco Bay Area, has written: 'Science and technology deal with things: atoms and galaxies, levers and micro-processors. The life of the spirit, on the other hand, deals with the connections between things: mercy, justice and love. We have become very good in the age of science and technology at knowing about things, but we're not really as wise as we should be at making connections' (*TIMELINE*, May/June 1996, p. 11).

Your workplace spirituality may well prompt you not only to be grateful for life, family, job and so many other gifts, but also to raise your head above the short-term chaos to notice that there are connections waiting to be made. You can make them. Helping others is the way to make those connections real.

Voluntary community service, whether spiritually motivated or not, is a civic responsibility. Someone has called it the 'rent' we have to pay for our citizenship. I've often thought that our judicial system has, without intending it, given community service a bad name.

Since the mid-1960s, offenders in some cases have been sentenced to a particular number of hours (usually in the thousands) of community service. I find it curious that we assign as a punishment in a judicial sentencing category an obligation that every good citizen was once expected to meet voluntarily. Perhaps 'compensatory service' would be a better term for courts to use in imposing a civil or criminal penalty to offset damage done to the community by a lawbreaker.

Your voluntary community service, rendered in the spirit of generosity, will have many benefits for yourself as well as for those you help. Biblical spirituality tells you that it is better to give than to receive. Helping others will convince you of the solid practical truth of that proposition.

In some instances, you will find yourself helping others overcome one of the setbacks you yourself have experienced. It may turn out that this will enable you to see, at long last, a reason for the reversal you suffered. Perhaps your unhappy experience prepared you to assist others. Of course, you don't have to set yourself up as a specialist in helping others over any one specific hump. Your best approach may be to keep yourself free and flexible to respond to opportunities to be of service whenever they arise.

INITIATIVES

Let me caution you to be your own centre of initiative in any recovery situation. I mean by this that you have to experience yourself as one *taking initiatives – not as a person acted upon by others*. This means that when others give you welcome assistance, you should be sure to take it, but you should never let them, however innocently and unwittingly, take control.

You can never afford to substitute outside help or helpers for yourself as the centre of initiative in your life. Nor should you ever permit yourself to occupy that centre in the life of someone you hope to help.

BEYOND SERVILITY

Contrary to the impression given by rugged individualists in fact or fiction, service (in all its forms) is not servility. Nor are service workers in any way intended to be second-class citizens. They are persons of unique value whose dignity is enlarged precisely because their vocation enables them to serve others. The focus of this chapter, however, is not on service employment, but on voluntary service.

Private voluntary service represents a special opportunity for you to enhance your sense of your own human dignity as it expands your appreciation of the dignity of those you serve. As in so many other suggestions offered in this book, you will never know that service works to your advantage, as well as to the advantage of those you serve, unless you give it a try.

Impressive statistics can be presented on the number of hours of volunteer service being offered by men and women of all ages today. Some are at the intersections of life where the needs are urgent; most are farther out on the periphery. All are necessary. Helping others can, of course, happen at home or at work; it doesn't have to be 'extra help' out in the community.

BEYOND DEAL-MAKING

Unhappiness at home or work often relates to a refusal to be voluntarily helpful to others there. Where an unwritten law of reciprocity ('I'll help you, if you help me', 'You go first and then I'll do my part') rules the home or workplace environment, all moves are measured and generosity is squeezed dry. Some people, I've observed, seem far more ready to be helpful out in the community than they are at home or work. They are hiding, not serving.

BEYOND FEAR

Overcoming some fear may be necessary before you are free enough to help. The fear of rejection is always there. The fear of bodily harm is sometimes associated with efforts to help impoverished people in very poor communities. The fear of not knowing what to say impedes some from volunteering to help the very ill.

Just as there is security in numbers, there is reassuring encouragement for the would-be volunteer if the work can be done with other volunteers. At least the going there and coming back parts of the experience can be structured in such a way that connects you to others and helps lower the level of fear.

I was impressed when college students who volunteered as tutors in a low-income, high-crime neighbourhood in Washington, DC, told me that they had no problem at all getting to and from their assignments on city buses, because they were always met at the bus stop by the illiterate men they were teaching how to read and write, and escorted back safely by these same appreciative pupils once the sessions were over.

I served for several years on the board of directors of what was originally called the Commission on National and Community Service (now the Corporation on National Service), a federal initiative begun in 1990 to encourage volunteer activity in America. Once at the urging of another board member, Richard F. ('Digger') Phelps, former basketball coach at the University of Notre Dame, the commission members went 'across the street', as Digger liked to put it, into a store-front church in a poverty neighbourhood in the District of Columbia. Our aim was to see some of the problems service initiatives there and around the country would, we hoped, be addressing.

Two women, members of a support group for mothers of youth killed in the drug wars, described the conditions that brought their sons to early graves and themselves to unrelenting grief. A streetsmart young man explained his willingness to risk arrest by dealing in drugs ('in order to get money, to get clothes, to get girls') and to use firepower in the street to defend himself whenever he and his supply were attacked ('I'd rather be tried by twelve than carried by six'). That was in 1992, when Malcom X came back to life on movie screens and the words of Martin Luther King were being widely quoted in many discussions (including ours) on community service as a neighbourhood rescue strategy. The youth, who had expressed a preference for a jury of twelve over six pallbearers, also remarked, 'Any community that has to look to dead men for role models is in real trouble'. Of course, he was right.

An older gentleman from that same neighbourhood, a participant in this same discussion and the father of two sons who had met violent deaths in the drug wars, commented: 'I'd rather be dead than be eighteen or nineteen today'.

The eighteen- and nineteen-year-olds in poor neighbourhoods, as well as countless people in lower and higher age brackets, and in neighbourhoods rich and poor, need the kind of help that generous, open-minded, and, yes, brave community service volunteers can provide. The spiritual principle of generosity, one of the Pauline Criteria, will point you in their direction. It is up to you to take the step.

The Book of Proverbs advises: 'He who has compassion on the poor lends to the Lord, and he will repay him for his good deed' (19:17). You have been encouraged earlier in this book to think of your spirituality as a savings account from which you can draw the strength you need to meet your day-by-day responsibilities. The help you freely give to others is a form of compassion. When you do this for the poor and needy, you are assured by the Book of Proverbs that you are 'lending' to God, who will repay this loan to your account at exponential rates of interest.

CHAPTER TWENTY
HOPE

The poet George Herbert expressed the encouraging idea that anyone 'who walks in hope dances without music'. Most of us have to make it through life without the benefit of background music. Whether you walk or dance, you make your way each day by even-paced measures without the tempo-enhancing encouragement of violins and trumpets. For many years, you have probably been absorbing from the cinema screen lessons about life that are cleverly (and often deceptively) wrapped in background music. Characters in the films have music to intensify their emotional highs, warn them (and the audience) of impending danger, or accelerate their slide into deeper despair. In those rare moments of emotional intensity when the music stops, you, the viewer, are left in a suspended state of watching and waiting, trying (often uncomfortably) to figure things out for yourself.

Real life is different. You can make your own movies, so to speak, by imagining what, and why, and how you will do what you are going to do today and in all your tomorrows. But you have to choose the attitude – the inner silent state of mind – that will accompany you (and serve as your 'accompaniment') along the way. If you want to walk in hope, you have to choose to do so.

THREE VIRTUES

Hope is one of three 'theological virtues', so named because each has God for its direct object. The other two are faith and charity. The object of each is God. Your faith is directed towards God; your hope is grounded in God; your charity (love) is aimed directly at God.

Your practice of these three virtues will have indirect effects on many other people. In consequence of your firm faith in God, you know how to be faithful to others. Full of unshakable hope that God's promises to you will be fulfilled, you can present yourself to others as a hopeful person, an anchor, a rock. Your unconditional love of God, for God's own goodness and not for what he has to give to you, enables you to convey something of the divine goodness to others in your own (by definition limited) acts of charity and love.

The one-act play title, *Hope is the Thing with Feathers*, has intrigued me since I first came across it in my college years. The play is a mixture of humour and pathos revolving around hobos trying to snatch a duck from a pond in New York City's Central Park. The suggestion in the title is, I imagine, that hope can flutter and fly away. My point would be that hope will flee *only if* you choose not to hang onto it. 'I don't think hope ever dies,' psychiatrist David Morrison once remarked to me; 'it is buried in many people, but it can surface again.'

Hope is not to be confused with optimism, which focuses always on 'the best'. 'Optimising' opportunities and achieving 'optimal' outcomes might be 'optimistically' regarded as part of 'the best' in the 'best of all worlds'. That is not the way it is with hope. Hope is a great deal closer to the human heart – hesitant or stout, weak or strong – and to the ground on which the have-a-heart person walks (or dances!).

Hope is inextricably bound up with expectation – and, of course, your expectations will often focus on things getting better than they are right now. This is not to suggest that hope comes into play only when things are bad. You don't have to be ill in order to get better. The situation does not have to be in a deplorable state in order to begin to improve. Expectation is the thrilling dimension of hope. Expectation is part of the stretch that is integral to your spirituality.

'HOPEFULLY'

I have no idea when the word 'hopefully' rose to the prominent place of misapplication that it now enjoys in the American vernacular. That adverb means 'in a happily expectant way'. If used correctly, it would describe a personal condition similar to the mood conveyed in expressions like 'proudly announce', or 'gladly welcome'. The misapplied 'hopefully' (for example, 'Hopefully, we will hear from them soon') really means, 'It is to be hoped that …'

This is more than a simple grammatical quibble. Most of the people I hear punctuating their conversations with the word 'hopefully' do not give all that much evidence of being all that hopeful!

The famous words from Dante's *Inferno* appear (figuratively) above the entrance to many workplaces; or at least they are written on the minds of many as they go to work: 'Abandon hope, all ye who enter here'. This is not the stuff of a sound and practical workplace spirituality.

Give yourself an 'expectations check-up' from time to time, to make sure that your supply, your savings account, of positive hopes is abundant. And realise that similar positive expectations are (or perhaps were) on the minds of your associates in the workplace. What were your hopes, your expectations, when you started out on this job? Achievement, money, fame, power, security, influence, creativity, satisfaction, the opportunity to serve, the chance to make your mark? All or some combination of the above? If you are like most other humans, few, if any, of your goals have been fully realised. And the shortfall may be attributable to one or several of the reversals or wounds catalogued earlier in this book. There's nothing unusual about this; it is all part of the human predicament.

How, then, do you cope? How do you keep your expectations high and positive? How do you keep your career and yourself in balance and on course into the future?

Hope is the only route to take. Remember, hope is a theological virtue; its object is God. Forge that link for yourself in prayer and everything else will fall into line.

HOPE AS A WORKPLACE ANCHOR

Never forget that you can make the God in whom you hope become present in your workplace – for the benefit of those with whom you work – simply by being hopeful. Your centred hopefulness (a quality not to be confused with blind, Pollyanna-inspired optimism) makes you an anchor, a rock for others, a source of serenity and stability. And, as is always the case in the realm of Christian spirituality, in providing this kind of help to others, you are also helping yourself.

You may think of this phenomenon as an example of what the French novelist George Bernanos called 'the miracle of the empty hands'. You, who stand in need of hope, are able to give it to others without necessarily feeling very hopeful yourself. And so it is with love, faith, trust and forgiveness: you can give what you think you do not have. In the realm of spirituality, at any rate, you can; this should serve to remind you where the power is, and has been, all along. A wonderful priest I once knew was fond of saying, 'Jesus promises you two things: your life will have meaning, and you're going to live forever. If you can find a better offer, take it'. Build your future on the durability of hope.

Hope is the pillar of the world. Because of it, you are a lot stronger than you think. It may surprise you to learn that John Updike once wrote, 'God is a bottomless encouragement to our faltering and frightened being'. It will not, I think, surprise you at all to know that the author of the Pauline Criteria said much the same thing centuries earlier in his letter to the Romans (5:3-5): '[W]e even boast of our afflictions, knowing that affliction produces endurance, and endurance, proven character, and proven character, hope, and hope does not disappoint, because the love of God has been poured out into our hearts through the holy Spirit that has been given to us.'

Your hope will surely never disappoint as long as the object of your hope is God. When your hopes appear to be 'dashed', consider the possibility that the God in whom you never stop hoping has something better in mind for you.

HOPE AS GUIDER AND SUSTAINER

Hope is always future-focused. It fuels your second starts. It sustains your journey through life, especially through life's final stages. Knowing, as you do, that 'all the world's a stage', you have to acknowledge your potential (even propensity) to 'act', and you have to check the face behind your mask. Are you truly a hopeful person?

What abiding hope can do for you was demonstrated beautifully by Cardinal Joseph Bernardin as his life ended in 1996. 'His way of death confirms that this man did not have two faces, one private, one public', said Rabbi Herman Schaalman, a longtime friend. 'He was inside with his outside, outside with his inside, which is rare.'

That rare quality is the fruit of a functioning spirituality. The ultimate answers come from within because your spiritual guidelines long ago found root there. Your inside becomes your outside in moments of challenge; you are able to face up to reality without losing either heart or hope.

The memorial card distributed to those who paid their respects at the wake services and funeral held in Chicago for Cardinal Bernardin in November 1996, had his picture on the front and the 'Prayer of St Francis' on the back. The Cardinal carried that prayer in his coat pocket every day and recited it often. 'Lord, make me an instrument of your peace', is the opening petition. Midway through a list of subsequent requests, you will find these words: 'Where there is despair, let me sow hope'. Every believer, I think, wants to do just that.

Take to heart these words from Simon Peter, the first pope: 'Always be ready to give an explanation to anyone who asks you for a reason for your hope' (1 Peter 3:15). He presumed, apparently, that the Christian believer would always be a puzzle to the world. Truth be told, if you are genuinely hopeful, you will puzzle many even today.

CHAPTER TWENTY-ONE
LOOKING UP

We say things are 'looking up' when light appears at the end of the tunnel, or when we have a sense of something positive about to enter our lives. The advice we often give to a discouraged friend is simply, 'Keep your chin up'. With the chin raised the outlook is also elevated.

A positive, upbeat attitude is an essential component of any recovery-and-rebound strategy. The 'attitude', as space-flight vocabulary reminds the world, is a leaning, a tilt. Your attitudinal tilt has to be forward and upward.

KEEPING THINGS IN FRONT – IF YOU CHOOSE TO
I remember being impressed by the response of a major American college basketball coach immediately after his team, ranked number three in the nation, was humiliated by a lower-ranked challenger just before 'March Madness', the rush to become one of the National Collegiate Athletic Association season-ending tournament's 'Final Four'. Without missing a beat, the coach told reporters, 'We are not going to put this one behind us; we'll keep it in front of us'. The spectacle of past mistakes and miscues would, he hoped, guide his team back to the top of the national rankings.

You have the option of putting your reversals completely behind you and looking resolutely up, or filtering your forward and upward gaze through the memory of the past. It is your choice. Use the past, but only if it helps. Wipe it out of your memory if it is preventing you from looking up and moving ahead.

One manager I know keeps his eye on four words from the pen of Emily Dickinson: 'I dwell in possibility'. This is the mantra that lifts his heart. The words were printed on a card a friend used some years ago to write him an encouraging note while he was in transition after an involuntary separation from a job he thought he could never lose. Those four words 'did it' for him, he said.

'Even now', he told me, 'I have the card, beaten and battered, pinned to the wall above my desk. I try to live up to its meaning as much as I can.' The meaning behind the idea of 'dwelling in possibility' is that no matter where you are in life, you are perched on a pillar of hope. Something good is about to happen. Just keep looking up so that, when it comes, you can see the 'possibility' that is ready to be realised right there in the circumstances where you now 'dwell'. And remember, dwelling in possibility beats dwelling in impossibility every time.

To dwell in possibility, look up and out, after you have taken your bearings from within, there are steps to be taken, a future to be met.

THE FUTURE

Sometimes, the 'future' is used as a subtle substitute for God. I say 'subtle' because it can slip into your outlook without even you noticing what is going on. Your speech will betray you when this happens. Be careful if you often hear yourself 'believing in the future', 'putting your trust in the future', 'feeling good about the future'. There is nothing wrong with any of that, unless the future is *all* you believe in or trust. First, believe in God; then yourself and your destiny. If your 'looking up' is anchored in God and rooted in the values you hold within, you can rest assured that the future will take care of itself. After all, your Lord, the Lord of the spirituality you've been considering in these pages, is also Lord of the past, present, *and future*. Trust him.

EXPERIENCE AND RESPONSIBILITY

Looking up does not, of course, mean looking away; it is not abdication of responsibility. Review the topics you've considered in this book. Some of them are still yours to deal with personally; you cannot pretend they are not there. Some of the other issues will no longer be problems for you, but other persons within your sphere of influence will have to deal with them and they may look to you for help. You cannot now hold your head in the air and ignore the challenges that others lay at your feet. This may be decision time.

You gave some thought to hope in the last chapter. Now you are 'looking up' (and out). Let Shakespeare's words condition your mind for a consideration of what you might want to do next:

> There is a tide in the affairs of men,
> Which, taken at the flood, leads on to fortune;
> Omitted, all the voyage of their life
> Is bound in shallows and in misery.
> On such a full sea are we now afloat;
> And we must take the current when it serves,
> Or lose our ventures.
> (*Julius Caesar*, Act IV, Scene iii)

There is a current you can take. No need to think of things on a grand 'affairs-of-men' scale. Keep the consideration on a manageable scale; match it up to your experiences, your needs, and your opportunities in light of all you've been through – and learned – thus far in life.

REVIEWING WHAT YOU'VE LEARNED
From where you find yourself at this very moment, think about criticism, fear, betrayal, false accusations, ingratitude, being passed over, layoff, prejudice, sexual harassment and personal mistakes. (You've been through a lot in these pages!) Then think about moving ahead.

All of these brushes with reality, all of these elements that are part of normal living, challenge the relevance of your faith to ordinary life and work. If faith cannot speak to you there, what good is faith for you? But now that you have had the opportunity to reflect and pray by the promptings you found on these pages, you know that faith can address all these issues ... and any others that may arise in your life.

You know that faith is good, and useful, and necessary for you. And you have an understanding now of how spirituality provides an infrastructure of support.

THE NINE CRITERIA REVISITED

A practical spirituality functions as a communications network, keeping you in touch with the source of all goodness and power. More specifically, each of the nine Pauline Criteria leads you to the source of all goodness and power.

The list, as you no doubt remember, begins with love. At the end of every experience of authentic love, you will find God, for 'God is love' (1 John 4:8). 'To love another person is to see the face of God', goes the secular proclamation of this same truth in the finale of the musical *Les Misérables*.

Joy is next. Remember that joy (not to be confused with mere lightheartedness or hilarity) tops the list of the Pauline Criteria that attest to the vibrancy of your spirituality. Joy, however, can come and go (or better, surface and recede). 'Gloom we will always have with us, a rank and sturdy weed,' writes Barbara Holland, 'but joy requires tending.' Tend to the cultivation of your own deep-down joy, your abiding happiness, and you will have prepared the solid ground on which your poised and balanced 'looking up' can stand secure.

Genuine joy cannot be described, only experienced. And the experience is not a sudden, surface eruption like laughter. Joy is something that has to be tended, nurtured, respected, even reverenced, because joy is the presence of God to the soul.

Peace, the objective of every soul's search, is a by-product of wisdom. 'The Lord by wisdom founded the earth', says the book of Proverbs (3:19), and wisdom's 'paths are peace'. Those who search for peace are searching, whether they know it or not, for the God of wisdom. Augustine knew this when he wrote: 'You have made us for yourself, O Lord, and our hearts are restless till they rest in you.'

Patience, you will remember, is another path to God. Who else but God can be there at the bottom of all reality? Your patience is your deepest possible acceptance of reality, your persevering acceptance of things as they are. Your patience does not foreclose the possibility of change; it expresses your obedience to the natural laws of growth and to the will of the God of all reality.

Kindness is in every instance a disclosure of what God is like. Your every kindness is an opportunity for the God who dwells within to have a presence, through you, in the places where your kindnesses are seen and felt. Similarly, kindnesses shown to you by others are expressions, through them, of God's love and care for you.

Generosity is another sign of God's presence. It functions like a two-way street that leads the generous person to God, who, as Paul testifies, 'loves a cheerful giver' (2 Corinthians 9:7), and it can bring God to any beneficiary of a generous act who is graced to see the ultimate giver behind the gift.

Faithfulness is *required* of the believer. God does not require that you be brave, or bright, or outstanding in anything but your faithfulness whereby you stand out, despite your doubts, before your God. The faith of your faithfulness is something that can be neither merited nor earned. It can only be given. And there is only One who can give the gift of faith. With that gift, you possess the God of faithfulness. All you can be is grateful.

Gentleness is the very atmosphere of divinity. If you are gentle, you are Godlike. If gentleness comes your way, you can find God in that breeze. And if your gentle soul is filled with faith, hope, and love; if veracity and forgiveness are there too, your gentle soul is as strong as steel. Gentleness is the strength of spiritual giants.

Self-control is a lever in your hand. Only you, with God's help, can turn it. God respects your freedom. You can freely decide not to throw the lever of self-control ... and that will mean permitting material excesses or spiritual pride to overrun your soul. Thus overrun, the soul is no longer fertile ground for the principles of spirituality. Weeds develop; there is no longer room in the soul for answers from within. Whenever you use that lever, though, you will find yourself clearing away the weeds and moving closer to the God who created the self that is now in your control.

With these nine tools and their associated ideas in your possession, you notice that things are looking up. You now know how to deal with the human predicament. It is all a matter of mixing faith with work and with the rest of the wonderful life that is yours. You dwell in infinite possibility. You can take the prophet Hosea at his inspired word:

> Let us know, let us strive to know the Lord;
>   as certain as the dawn is his coming,
>   and his judgment shines forth like the light of day!
> He will come to us like the rain,
>   like spring rain that waters the earth. (Hosea 6:3)

ACKNOWLEDGEMENTS

My thanks to Theresa Murtha, former Vice-President and Publisher of the Macmillan Consumer Information Group, and to Dick Staron, Editor-in-Chief of Business and Finance Publications at Macmillan, who saw the need for a book like this and invited me to write it. Dick managed this project in its original stage and was extraordinarily helpful. I'm grateful also to Brandon Toropov for his interest and excellent copy-editing. Macmillan published this book in 1998 and then permitted it, as they say in the publishing business, to 'go out of print'. Happily for me and, I hope, for another wave of readers in Ireland, the UK, and USA, Donna Doherty of Veritas Publications invited me to cooperate with Veritas in bringing the book, in revised, shortened, and updated form, back into print. Skillful editing by Catherine Gough guided the entire process.

Mike and Pat Snell, of the Snell Literary Agency in Truro, Massachusetts, have a great sense for right organisation and progression in a project like this; their suggestions and encouragement helped a lot.

My friend John Fontana introduced me to his colleagues David Morrison and David Deacon, of Morrison Associates in Pallatine, Illinois. Their approach to business consulting is unusual, if not unique, and extraordinarily useful. John and both Davids were generous in offering me insights and the benefit of their considerable experience with workplace issues. John Fontana also offered helpful comments on the finished manuscript.

As a member of the Woodstock Business Conference, a network of American business managers who want to explore the relevance of their religious faith to business practice, I've participated in many rich discussions and much prayerful reflection on workplace spirituality. My Jesuit friend Jim Connor, former director of the Woodstock Theological Centre at Georgetown University and organiser of the Woodstock Business Conference, which has chapters in about fifteen American cities, read the manuscript and provided helpful suggestions.

Many others offered anecdotes, reflections and general encouragement; I'm grateful to them all. This topic is alive today in the minds of these and countless other faith-committed people. As they work, they are all searching for a deeper meaning in what they are 'doing'. I expect to continue to learn much more from them on the relevance of faith to work, and I hope what they find in this book will offer them some encouragement in return.

WJB